Japanese Fortified Temples and Monasteries AD 710–1602

Stephen Turnbull • Illustrated by Peter Dennis

Series editors Marcus Cowper and Nikolai Bogdanovic

First published in Great Britain in 2005 by Osprey Publishing,
Midland House, West Way, Botley, Oxford OX2 0PH, UK
443 Park Avenue South, New York, NY 10016, USA
Email: info@ospreypublishing.com

A CIP catalogue record for this book is available from the British Library

ISBN 1 84176 826 X

Editor: Ilios Publishing, Oxford, UK (www.iliospublishing.com)
Index by Alison Worthington
Maps by The Map Studio Ltd
Originated by United Graphics, Singapore
Printed in China through Bookbuilders.

05 06 07 08 09   10 9 8 7 6 5 4 3 2 1

FOR A CATALOGUE OF ALL BOOKS PUBLISHED BY OSPREY MILITARY AND AVIATION
PLEASE CONTACT:

NORTH AMERICA
Osprey Direct, 2427 Bond Street, University Park, IL 60466, USA
E-mail: info@ospreydirectusa.com

ALL OTHER REGIONS
Osprey Direct UK, P.O. Box 140 Wellingborough, Northants, NN8 2FA, UK
E-mail: info@ospreydirect.co.uk

www.ospreypublishing.com

Dedication

To my grandson Joseph Alexander Turnbull, born on 16 October
2004, the day I finished this book.

Artist's note

Readers may care to note that the original paintings from which
the colour plates in this book were prepared are available for
private sale. All reproduction copyright whatsoever is retained by
the Publishers. All enquiries should be addressed to:

Peter Dennis, The Park, Mansfield, Notts, NG18 2AT

The Publishers regret that they can enter into no correspondence
upon this matter.

Acknowledgements

I would particularly like to thank the curators and staff of Osaka
City Museum of History; Osaka Castle Museum; Namba Betsuin,
Osaka; Enryakuji; Yoshizakiji and the Rennyo Shonin Kinenkan in
Yoshizaki and the Ikko-ikki Museum, Torigoe. I also thank Nahoko
Kitajima for her help in arranging my access to Nishi Honganji.

Preface

For almost 1,000 years the samurai, Japan's warrior aristocracy,
dominated its society and its politics. From the central
government of the *shogun*, the military dictator, down to the local
daimyo (warlords) who fought each other for territory, the main
power was always in the hands of those who controlled armies
and fought with spears, swords and guns. Courtiers, merchants
and farmers alike were forced to bow to the wishes of the
samurai.

On certain occasions challenges were mounted against
samurai rule. Twice in Japan's history emperors, who were
required to behave merely as religious figureheads, led
unsuccessful revolts; but the most serious and sustained
opposition came from organizations whose loyalties centred on
commonly held religious beliefs. In the 11th and 12th centuries
these were the *sohei* (warrior monks) located in the huge
monastery complexes of Hieizan (Mount Hiei) and Nara. Their
activities were greatly curtailed as a result of the Gempei Wars of
1180–85, but warrior monk temples survived to provide fresh
military challenges as late as the 16th century.

From the mid-15th century onwards the *sohei*'s role as the
militant opponents of the samurai class was almost eclipsed by
the rise of populist Buddhist movements among the lower classes
of society. Of these the most important were the adherents of
Jodo Shinshu (the True Pure Land sect), otherwise known as the
Ikko-shu (single-minded sect). This tended to be the name used
by their opponents, and was abandoned during the Meiji
Restoration. Jodo Shinshu's armies, however, are known to history
as the Ikko-ikki (the single-minded league).

In this book I shall examine the fortified Buddhist temples
and monasteries of the warrior monks and their successors,
showing how they sustained their armies and defended
themselves during some of the most savage campaigns in Japanese
history. I shall also show how the fortified Buddhist sites
anticipated the later development of the Japanese castle.
Nowhere is this more apparent than in the creation of *jinaimachi*
(temple towns) that developed round the fortified temples of
Osaka and elsewhere. They attracted merchants and craftsmen
and grew to be important urban centres. As such they were the
forerunners of the *jokamachi* (castle towns) that were to become
such a prominent feature of Japanese life from the early 17th
century onwards.

The Fortress Study Group (FSG)

The object of the FSG is to advance the education of the public in
the study of all aspects of fortifications and their armaments,
especially works constructed to mount or resist artillery. The FSG
holds an annual conference in September over a long weekend
with visits and evening lectures, an annual tour abroad lasting
about eight days, and an annual Members' Day.

The FSG journal *FORT* is published annually, and its newsletter
Casemate is published three times a year. Membership is
international. For further details, please contact:

The Secretary, c/o 6 Lanark Place, London W9 1BS, UK

Editor's note

Unless otherwise indicated, all the images in this book are the
property of the author.

Contents

From worshippers to warriors – the development of the fortified temple

Sohei and *monto*

The reference in the Preface to the existence of *jinaimachi* (temple towns), which were very well defended as part of the overall environment of a religious community, begs the question as to the true identity of the inhabitants of the fortified temples and monasteries for whom the expression 'warrior monk' is often used. This is the popular translation of the word *sohei*, which literally means 'priest soldier', and refers to the armies maintained by the monasteries of Hieizan and Nara from about AD 970 until the 16th century. It can also be applied to the Shingon temple called Negorodera in Kii Province. A helpful comparison is with the military religious orders of Europe that emerged during the Crusades. Indeed, this provided a useful analogy for the only European visitor ever to make their acquaintance, the Jesuit missionary Father Caspar Vilela, who visited Negorodera early in the 1560s and described its adherents as being like the Knights of St John.

The populist Jodo Shinshu communities, however, were very different, and to describe the *monto* (believers) of Jodo Shinshu as 'warrior monks' is highly misleading. Their communities attracted samurai, farmers and townsmen in associations of shared religious beliefs led by ordained priests. The Ikko-ikki, as the armies of Jodo Shinshu were known, were certainly warriors but never warrior monks. In fact the teachings of Shinran (1173–1262), with whom the

The *goeido mon* (founder's gate) of Higashi Honganji, the present-day headquarters in Kyoto of the Otani branch of the Honganji, the 'original vow' temple of Jodo Shinshu. This immense gate was built in 1911.

The Jodo Shinshu temple of Koshoji. It is located in the historic *jinaimachi* (temple town) quarter of Tondabayashi, a town near Osaka.

sect originated, had revolutionized Japanese Buddhism by doing away with the duality of monasticism and laity and replacing it with a new emphasis on spiritual egalitarianism. So rather than comparing the Ikko-ikki to the Knights of Rhodes, a better European analogy would be the Hussites of Bohemia or the extreme Puritan communities that arose a century later during the Reformation. Linked by zeal for their beliefs, and under the leadership of charismatic preachers, they formed self-governing communities defended by armies. So it was with Jodo Shinshu and their fortified temples.

The rise of the warrior monks

The original Buddhist priest soldiers were formed as a result of the rivalries that existed between the temples of Nara, the old capital of Japan, and of Hieizan, the mountain that lay near to Kyoto, the city that replaced Nara as capital in AD 894. The great temples of Nara such as Todaiji and Kofukuji resented the move to Kyoto, and were particularly jealous of Enryakuji, the temple that was located on the summit of Hieizan. There were also major arguments over the right of the Hieizan clergy to ordain new monks instead of this being performed exclusively in Nara.

Sohei of the late 16th century, indicated by the inclusion of a gun, are shown here defending their temple using portable wooden shields.

The first major incident of violence involving priests happened in AD 949. It began as a protest demonstration by a delegation from Todaiji to Kyoto, and ended with a brawl during which some of the participants lost their lives. Other incidents followed, so, in about AD 970 Ryogen, the *zasu* (chief priest) of Enryakuji made the decision to create a permanent fighting force to defend Hieizan and its growing wealth. These men soon became involved in inter-temple disputes, some of which were fought between Enryakuji, and its daughter temple Onjoji, or Miidera, which lay at the foot of Hieizan. Over the next 100 years there are references to fighting between Enryakuji, Miidera and the temples of Nara. By 1006 the Kofukuji of Nara could field an army numbering some 3,000 *sohei*. There were also several instances when *sohei* marched down to Kyoto to place their demands in front of members of the imperial court, whom the *sohei* intimidated as much with their curses as they did with their weapons.

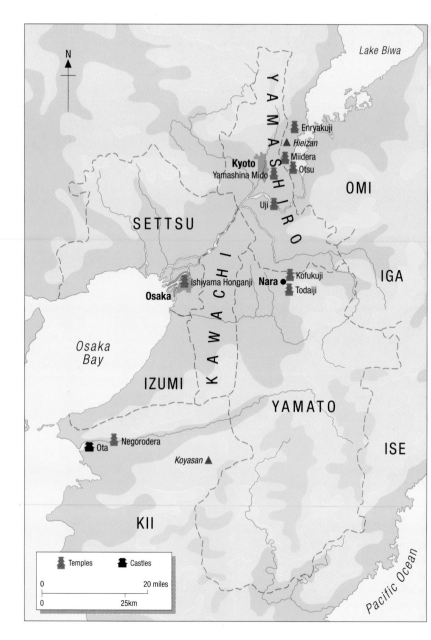

There were no permanent fortifications associated with these *sohei* sites. The Enryakuji was defended solely by its position on a high wooded mountain. The temples of Nara were more open to assault, and were forced to erect temporary fortifications when they were faced with attack in 1181. This was at the start of the Gempei Wars, a struggle for supremacy between the samurai families of Taira and Minamoto. The *sohei* involvement was brief, tragic and almost totally destructive of them as an entity. The monks of Miidera supported the imperial claimant put forward by the Minamoto family, but were heavily defeated at the first battle of Uji in 1180 as they were heading south from Kyoto to join up with their fellow *sohei* from Nara. The victorious Taira took terrible retribution, and after a desultory defence Miidera was burned to the ground. in 1181 the Taira burned down most of the buildings in Nara, including Todaiji and its huge statue of Buddha. The destruction of Nara was such a shock to the priests of Hieizan, who had been standing aloof from the conflict, that there was almost no more *sohei* activity for the rest of the Gempei Wars.

Minamoto Yoritomo, the victor in the Gempei Wars, became the first *shogun* (military dictator) of Japan and established the principle of samurai rule. His religious sensibilities, however, encouraged him to rebuild the Nara temples, and it was not long before the monks rediscovered their military skills. In 1221 we read of warrior monks from Nara being involved in the brief Shokyu War. Monks from Hieizan fought in the Nanbokucho Wars of the 14th century, and were active until their final destruction in 1571.

Jodo Shinshu and the first fortified temple

Around about the time of the Shokyu War an important new development was taking place in Japanese Buddhism through the teachings of Shinran, who founded Jodo Shinshu, the 'True Pure Land Sect'. The new sect's beliefs contrasted sharply with the monastic approach of the older institutions of Nara and Kyoto and proved highly attractive to the lower orders of society. Its features included local membership centred around village meeting places, a charismatic leadership under the headship of Shinran's lineal descendants, who were free to marry, and a fundamental independence from traditional regimes, whether aristocratic or military. In 1272 Shinran's daughter Kakushin-ni (1221–81) built the Otani mausoleum in Kyoto to house the ashes of her father, and in 1321 Shinran's great-grandson Kakunyo (1270–1351) converted it into the first Honganji, the 'temple of the original vow'. From then on the expression 'Honganji' came to refer not only to the building that was its headquarters, but to the dominant Honganji-led faction in Jodo Shinshu. At Otani Honganji, Kakunyo began to develop the ideas of Shinran into a coherent religious system.

In spite of it being the location of the grave of Shinran, recognition and power came very slowly to Otani Honganji during the first century and a half of its existence. Much of Shinran's original missionary work had been in the Kanto provinces, the area around modern-day Tokyo, so the Kanto temples such as Sensuji in Takada in Shimotsuke Province were unwilling to defer to the wishes of the Honganji. All was to change with the tenure of Rennyo (1415–99), the eighth head of the Honganji and Jodo Shinshu's great revivalist.

The second half of the 15th century, when Rennyo led the Honganji, was a time of great instability in Japan. The Ashikaga family had ruled Japan as *shogun* for over a century, but their tenure had become dominated by the petty quarrels of the *shugo*, the governors of a province or a group of provinces. The weakness of and divisions within the Shogunate came to a disastrous climax with the outbreak of the Onin War in 1467. Japan's capital city of Kyoto was the main battleground, and by the time the fighting ended in 1477 most of the city lay in ruins. The original cause of the conflict had been a succession dispute within the Shogunate, but by 1477 that had become an irrelevance with the shogun rendered almost powerless to control the course of events. Worse still, the fighting had spread to the provinces, as erstwhile *shugo* fought for supremacy and territory. Some succeeded in transforming themselves into independent feudal lords, for which the term *daimyo* (literally 'great name') is used. But former *shugo* were not the only *daimyo* around. Many more of them were military opportunists who had taken their chances and created petty kingdoms of their own. The century during which they fought each other is known by analogy with Chinese history as the *Sengoku Jidai* (The Warring States Period).

One consequence of the breakdown of law and order was that the lower orders of society were no longer content to be

Rennyo Shonin (1415–99), the great reformer and revivalist of Jodo Shinshu, the sect that created so many of the fortified temples of Japan.

ruled by an impotent *shogun* or an ambitious *shugo*. Instead, groups of peasants and low-ranking samurai used the weakness of established authority to assert their own autonomy. Popular uprisings and riots became a common feature of the times. They ranged from local disturbances to province-wide revolts, incidents that were generally referred to as *ikki* (riots), the original use of the word that was later used to designate those who took part in them. Into this turmoil walked Rennyo and his Jodo Shinshu followers, who were to contribute to the political history of Japan in a way that none of them could have envisaged.

Rennyo's personal charisma and his effectiveness as a preacher and proselytizer go a long way to explain why the Honganji branch of Jodo Shinshu grew at the expense of other factions. But there was another factor involved, and the stimulus came, ironically, from the warrior monks of Enryakuji. They were enraged by the influence that Otani Honganji was having on their traditional control of the religious life of the capital, so in 1465 an army of *sohei* descended upon Otani Honganji and burned it to the ground. Rennyo escaped from their clutches and took refuge with a few followers in nearby Wakasa Province. Not long afterwards the Hieizan monks pursued him there, but were attacked and driven off by the local Honganji members. This was the first manifestation of the military capabilities of the Jodo Shinshu *monto* that would make them so feared in the years to come.

In 1471, to put even greater distance between himself and the warrior monks of Hieizan, Rennyo moved to Yoshizaki in Echizen Province on the coast of the Sea of Japan. The area had already been thoroughly evangelized by Rennyo's uncle, so Rennyo was enthusiastically welcomed by the local *monto*. They helped him to build a new headquarters called Yoshizaki Gobo, which was completed in just three months. Here Rennyo produced some of his most important writings. He encouraged the local believers to set up *ko* (fraternities) that would not only be prayer organizations but would lay the foundations of future self-governing communities. But Yoshizaki Gobo was not just a Jodo Shinshu temple. It was built on a defensible plateau overlooking the sea, and Rennyo personally attended to the details of its fortification. He also urged the *monto* to be prepared for unhesitating sacrifice in defence of their faith. The first permanently fortified temple in Japan had been created.

Although Rennyo made it clear to his followers that resort to arms was justified only in the most extreme cases where the survival of Jodo Shinshu was at stake, to fortify a temple was a radical departure from the original teachings of Shinran, who had simply advocated moving to another place in the event of persecution. But this was the *Sengoku Jidai*. Unfortunately, although Rennyo's attitude was realistic, it left his organization open to possible abuse by militant *monto* who saw the ideological and military strength of the Honganji as a way of advancing their interests. Rennyo soon became alarmed by the belligerence shown by some *monto* who, incited by militant priests, began to attack other sects and challenge the civil authorities. Membership of Jodo Shinshu also proved attractive for low-ranking members of the samurai class who were able to combine their own small

A drawing of 1847 showing Yoshizaki. Yoshizaki Gobo, which lay on the plateau, had by this time been replaced by the temple buildings at its foot. These buildings still exist to this day.

forces under a common banner to produce an effective army. The pacifist Rennyo viewed all samurai with distaste, and wrote on one occasion that they were the 'enemies of Buddhism', but increasing numbers of samurai became *monto*. Their fighting skills were to prove useful in the years to come, with very dramatic results.

The Ikko-ikki take control of Kaga

The great breakthrough for the *monto* of Yoshizaki came from the direction of the neighbouring province of Kaga, where the Kaga Ikko-ikki came into being, not to defend the Jodo Shinshu faith per se but to assist a second-rate daimyo regain his position. In a long campaign (described in detail in Osprey's Elite 125: *Samurai Commanders (1) AD 940–1576* by the same author), the Ikko-ikki ousted the Togashi family and took over the province themselves. They ruled Kaga for the next 100 years in a unique demonstration of 'people power'.

In spite of this success, Rennyo feared that the Ikko-ikki of Yoshizaki would now be known for their military activities rather than for their religious lives. He was informed that the *sohei* of Hieizan had quietened down, so he decided to return to Kyoto, where in 1478 he founded Yamashina Mido. It was completed after five years of work and became his new headquarters. Sources tell of Yamashina Mido being of 'unsurpassed magnificence', and it was likened to the Jodo (Pure Land) itself. Like Yoshizaki Gobo, Yamashina Mido had to be fortified, but it would be many years before it had to face any attack.

The founding of Ishiyama Honganji

Kyoto's Yamashina Mido was completed in 1483. In spite of some residual rivalry, particularly from the Takada Sensuji in the Kanto, Rennyo had effectively realized the unfulfilled aspirations of his ancestor Kakunyo in making the Honganji the undisputed centre of Jodo Shinshu and the authority for the authentic teaching of Shinran.

Rennyo was now nearing the end of his life, but did not lack descendants to carry on his work, for he left 15 daughters and 13 sons, the last born when he was 84 years of age. So, with his succession secure Rennyo retired in 1489 and handed over the headship of the Honganji to his son Jitsunyo. Rennyo spent the first few years of his retirement within the compound of Yamashina Mido, but in 1496 he began to yearn for solitude, so he built a hermitage on a sweeping bend in the Yodo River downstream from Kyoto. It lay on a long, sloping, wooded plateau, and the 'long slope' gave the place its name: Osaka. A contemporary account noted how Rennyo had established his chapel 'on Ikutama manor, at a place called Osaka'; the first documented use of the name of what is now Japan's second city.

Osaka provided tranquillity for only a short time, however, because even in retirement Rennyo commanded a huge and loyal following. Thousands flocked to pay homage to him, so his simple hermitage was soon replaced by great prayer halls, residences for visiting Jodo Shinshu priests and extensive gardens. The growing complex was surrounded by formidable moats and walls. Tradesmen moved in, and by the time of Rennyo's death in 1499 the new foundation, now called Ishiyama Honganji, was beginning to take on its final shape. By the 1520s at least six residential neighbourhoods had grown up around the religious complex. Jodo Shinshu continued to grow and prosper under Shonyo, the tenth leader of the Honganji, who took over following his father Jitsunyo's death in 1525. Shonyo had friends in very high places, and in 1528 he was adopted into the family of an imperial regent. Such connections were to prove highly valuable in the turbulent years that lay ahead.

In spite of the growth of Osaka, Kyoto's Yamashina Mido was still regarded as the sect headquarters until a dramatic incident occurred. By the early 16th century Kyoto had become the city of a rising urban class who were rebuilding their capital from the ashes of the Onin War. Most of these merchant families

A group of worshippers entering Ishiyama Honganji's *goeido* through the main doorway. They remove their footwear at the bottom of the wooden staircase and proceed upwards across the balcony, over an inner corridor and through the open hinged doors. All eyes are drawn towards the central image of Amida. This is part of a model of Ishiyama Honganji's *goeido* in the Osaka City Museum of History.

were adherents of the Nichiren sect of Buddhism, otherwise known as the Hokkeshu or Lotus Sect. Jodo Shinshu and Nichirenshu had much in common in terms of their defensive mentality, but they were complete opposites when it came to recruitment. Jodo Shinshu was largely drawn from peasants and country samurai, while Nichirenshu appealed to the townspeople. There were 21 Nichiren temples in Kyoto, and their members organized themselves by neighbourhoods for self-protection and mutual regulation.

During the 15th century, spontaneous peasant mobs had frequently attacked the city, but by the 1530s similar attacks were being carried out by the Ikko-ikki, who had turned to militancy in much the same way as their comrades in Kaga had done. In 1532 Shonyo showed his personal belligerence by leading an attack against Kenponji, one of the main Nichiren centres in the port of Sakai. Following on from this success the Ikko-ikki even burned Kofukuji in Nara, one of the traditional centres of the *sohei*, and ransacked the Kasuga shrine. News of the destruction caused considerable apprehension within Kyoto when it was rumoured that the capital was the next target, but the Nichirenshu members rallied round the flag of the Holy Lotus and, after some initial setbacks, fought off an Ikko-ikki assault. Much aggrieved, the Nichiren believers decided to retaliate against the Ikko-ikki. They were not lacking in sympathetic samurai allies, and towards the end of 1532 they joined forces with Hosokawa Harumoto and Rokkaku Sadayori in an attack on Yamashina Mido, which they thoroughly sacked and burned. Shonyo was forced to take refuge in Ishiyama Honganji.

The abandonment of Yamashina Mido and the flight of Shonyo resulted in Ishiyama Honganji becoming the sect's headquarters for the next 50 years. Its strength was soon tested, because Hosokawa Harumoto and the Nichirenshu attacked it in 1533. To the great relief of the Ikko-ikki their massive temple complex, set within a natural moat of rivers and sea, withstood the assault and indeed appeared to be impregnable. This welcome demonstration of its strength and safety encouraged further commercial settlement, and the surrounding merchant community experienced considerable growth over the next few years. Ishiyama Honganji's wealth increased, and in 1536 the priests of the Honganji even paid all the expenses for the enthronement of Emperor Go Nara. It proved to be money well spent, because in 1538, the leaders of Ishiyama Honganji negotiated a deal with the imperial court and the local military governor to make the surrounding merchant community into a *jinaimachi* (temple town), with immunity from debt moratoriums and from entry by outside military forces.

A *jinaimachi* had been developed in Yoshizaki, but Osaka was to eclipse it both in size and concept. The Osaka *jinaimachi* area was officially recognized as being within the Ishiyama Honganji compound, so the Honganji levied its own land tax from the inhabitants and provided all their police and judicial functions as well as their spiritual and military needs. The self-contained community was such as success that by the middle of the 16th century a dozen or so smaller but similar *jinaimachi* had arisen in the provinces of Settsu, Kawachi and Izumi that now make up the modern metropolitan district of Osaka. All of them were commercial and military strongpoints defended by walls and ditches, and each had obtained from the outside authorities a package of self-governing privileges 'just like Osaka's'. The days of the Ikko-ikki as a simple rural peasant army had passed into history.

A few years later the Osaka communities benefited unexpectedly from the destruction of their Nichiren rivals in Kyoto. The attacks on the Nichiren temples by Ishiyama Honganji had continued until 1535, but when the final blow came it was struck not by Jodo Shinshu but by the old guard of the *sohei* of Hieizan. In 1536, by means of a raid of a type that Kyoto had not experienced for centuries, the warrior monks did the Ikko-ikki's work for them. All 21 major temples of the Lotus Sect were burned to the ground, taking much of their surroundings with them. The *sohei* spared the area around the imperial palace and the *shogun*'s headquarters, but the collateral damage was considerable.

While these developments were taking place in Kyoto and Osaka, the triumphant Ikko-ikki of Kaga had been suffering a series of factional disputes that eventually resulted in a civil war in 1531. The leadership of the Honganji faction proved victorious, and grew richer through confiscation of land, much of which was returned to the defeated factional members as fiefs when they pledged loyalty to the Honganji. The result was that by 1546 the sect's responsibilities in Kaga had become so great that it had to create a permanent local headquarters within the province. The site they chose became known as Oyama Gobo and was the beginning of the city of Kanazawa. Its population numbered between 3,000 and 5,000 people. From this headquarters the leaders of the Kaga Ikko-ikki ruled their province in a manner that any *daimyo* would have recognized, and many would have envied. On one occasion they fought the powerful Uesugi Kenshin to a standstill and blocked his access to the capital. Not bad for a *hyakusho no motaru kuni* ('a province ruled by peasants'), to use a popular phrase.

The Oyama Gobo, like the other branches of Jodo Shinshu, still recognized Ishiyama Honganji as its head and Shonyo as the leader. When Shonyo died in 1554 he was succeeded by his 11-year-old son Kennyo, who proved to be the most militant of all the Honganji leaders. Cometh the hour, cometh the man, because Kennyo was soon to face the fiercest onslaught in all of the Honganji's history.

Challenge to the Honganji

The 1560s and 1570s in Japan were dominated by the personality of one man: Oda Nobunaga (1534–82), who began the process of reunification of Japan. As a brilliant and ruthless general, Nobunaga's rise to power had begun with his surprise victory at the battle of Okehazama in 1560. More success followed, and in 1568 he entered the capital to set up his nominee Ashikaga Yoshiaki as *shogun*. But relations with Yoshiaki soon deteriorated and Nobunaga dismissed him, so the dispossessed *shogun* sought allies elsewhere. They included the Ikko-ikki.

Up to this point Nobunaga's victims had been rival *daimyo*, but in 1570 he experienced his first clash with the Ikko-ikki after Kennyo issued a call to arms. Nobunaga was fighting Miyoshi Yoshitsugu near Osaka when forces from

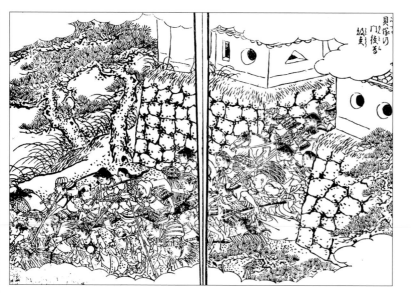

Ishiyama Honganji, including 3,000 armed with arquebuses, reinforced the Miyoshi and forced Nobunaga to withdraw. Soon afterwards they struck a more personal blow. The previous year, Oda Nobunaga had placed his brother Nobuoki in charge of Ogie Castle in Owari Province. In the 11th lunar month of 1570 the Ikko-ikki of the Nagashima delta took advantage of Nobunaga's departure for northern Omi and attacked Ogie, forcing Nobuoki to commit suicide. That same winter of 1570/71, when Nobunaga was driving back the Asai and Asakura armies, his flank was attacked by *sohei* from Enryakuji.

Warriors of the Ikko-ikki leave their fortified temple, which has gun ports in its walls.

The threat to Nobunaga from Ishiyama Honganji and its allies was not just one of actual fighting. It was also strategic and economic, because the power base of the Ikko-ikki coincided precisely with Nobunaga's own primary sphere of interest. The sect was particularly well entrenched within its fortified temples of Owari, Mino and Ise, the places where Nobunaga's own regime had been born. It lay across every approach to the capital save the west, from where the sympathetic *daimyo* Mori Motonari happily supported and supplied them from his coastal base. But the creation of *jinaimachi* had also lifted Jodo Shinshu from its peasant roots into a position of economic power, so that the Ishiyama Honganji could confront Nobunaga on commercial terms as well. It is therefore no exaggeration to say that the greatest challenge Nobunaga faced lay with the Ikko-ikki and their allies.

In must have seemed to Oda Nobunaga in 1571 that he was totally surrounded by religious fanatics, and when the time came to hit back he began with an easy target. In an operation so one-sided that it does not deserve the appellation of a battle, his troops moved against the *sohei* of Hieizan. In an orgy of fire and slaughter the samurai moved steadily up the mountain, killing everyone and everything in their way. No religious sensibilities stood in the way of the total destruction of the Hieizan temples. The threat to Nobunaga's flank was neutralized, and the long history of the Hieizan *sohei* came to a bloody end.

As for the Ikko-ikki, a long and bitter war had now started that was to last until Nobunaga's death 12 years later. He also brought some subtle politics into the equation that was to have an indirect effect on the development of the fortified temple. First, he pursued a policy of disarming the rural population from which the Ikko-ikki had traditionally drawn their strength. This went a long way towards separating the farming class from the samurai class, a development that is usually regarded as having begun with Toyotomi Hideyoshi's 'Sword Hunt' of 1588. So, for example, in 1575, when the Ikko-ikki of Echizen had been subdued, we read of regulations forbidding peasants to seek new masters or to leave their villages and ordering them to confine themselves to tilling the soil. In 1576 Nobunaga's General Shibata Katsuie conducted a Sword Hunt of his own in Echizen, just to make sure.

Secondly, Nobunaga made clever use of religious rivalry. It was not too difficult to persuade the Nichiren temples of Echizen to oppose the Ikko-ikki, but Nobunaga also made use of the jealousy that still existed between the Honganji and the smaller rival branches of Jodo Shinshu. Any Honganji *monto* who survived his attacks were given the opportunity to change their allegiance. For example, a surviving letter from Nobunaga to the Senpukuji in Mino Province in 1572 gives the temple two days to renounce its affiliation to Osaka. Similarly, the three Takada faction temples of Echizen were promised protection if they would publicly acknowledge their difference from Osaka and provide 'loyal service'. It proved to be a successful policy, because some *monto* from the Takada faction in Echizen went so far as to capture and kill Shimotsuma Hokkyo, one of the Ishiyama Honganji's principal deputies in that province.

The last stand of the Ikko-ikki

Oda Nobunaga's first campaign against Ishiyama Honganji was launched in August 1570. His last campaign against it finished in August 1580 after exactly ten years of intermittent but bitter fighting that involved many features beyond siege-work and assault. Both sides made considerable political efforts and a prolonged naval campaign was designed to cut the supply lines until, isolated from any support, Ishiyama Honganji eventually surrendered. On the night that it capitulated, the entire complex burst into flames and was utterly destroyed, probably on the initiative of the Ikko-ikki leaders themselves, who did not wish their glorious headquarters to become a prize for the man they had defied for so long.

Oda Nobunaga (1534–82), deadly enemy of the Ikko-ikki and their fortified temples. This is a detail from the statue of Nobunaga on the site of his castle of Kiyosu.

Nobunaga's war against the Ikko-ikki is commonly regarded as having finished with the surrender of Ishiyama Honganji in 1580. However, there were a few more years of bitter fighting left, and the first action was to be directed against Kaga Province. As early as 1573, forces commanded by Akechi Mitsuhide and Toyotomi Hideyoshi had driven through Echizen and on into the southern part of Kaga. In 1574 a fierce counter-attack by the Ikko-ikki blunted this advance, so Nobunaga took personal command of the response. In

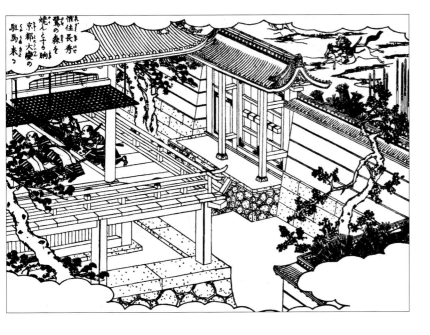

A rare illustration of a fortified temple in *Ehon Toyotomi Gunki*, an illustrated biography of Toyotomi Hideyoshi. It depicts a temple fortress called Saginomori, which was besieged by Niwa Nagahide in 1582.

The fortified temples of the Ikko-ikki, and Oda Nobunaga's campaigns against them from 1569 to 1582. (© Osprey Publishing Ltd)

1575 he left his base at Tsuruga and swept through Echizen, recapturing the province from Ikko-ikki forces. Mitsuhide and Hideyoshi then continued their advance into Kaga, taking in rapid succession the three fortified temples of Daishoji, Hinoya and Sakumi. By the end of 1575, the year that also saw Nobunaga's celebrated victory at Nagashino, the southern half of Kaga was firmly under Nobunaga's control and the Ikko-ikki federation was beginning to fall apart. In November 1575 Nobunaga boasted to the *daimyo* Date Terumune that he had 'wiped out several tens of thousands of the villainous rabble in Echizen and Kaga'.

Nobunaga assigned the newly pacified Echizen Province to Shibata Katsuie; one of his most trusted and experienced generals. In 1576 Katsuie's nephew Sakuma Morimasa advanced deeper into Kaga and captured Miyukizuka (modern-day Komatsu). Four years later, as the spearhead of his uncle's forces, Sakuma Morimasa devastated the Ikko-ikki of Kaga by destroying their headquarters of Oyama Gobo in Kanazawa.

In that same year of 1580 the Osaka Ishiyama Honganji surrendered. The war in Kaga should have been over, but diehard elements among the Ikko-ikki

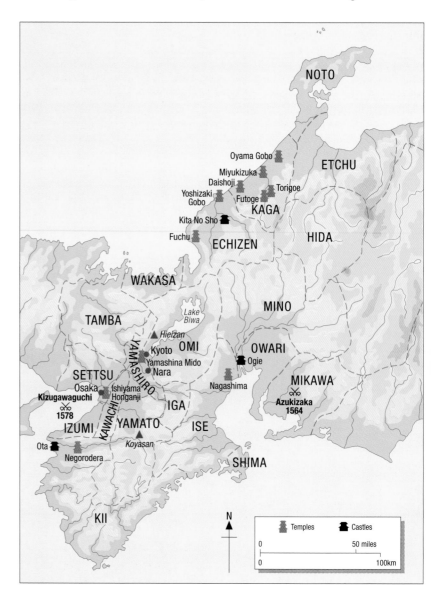

14

abandoned the flat plains of Kaga and entrenched themselves in fortified temples in the mountainous areas nearby. The most important locations were two sites in the foothills of the mighty Hakuzan mountains. They were called Torigoe and Futoge and were located on top of forested hills on either side of the river valley of the Dainichigawa, a branch of the Tedorigawa. The sites were to change hands three times within the following two years until these final outposts of the Kaga Ikko-ikki were wiped out.

Oda Nobunaga died in 1582, and three years later his successor, Toyotomi Hideyoshi finally quelled militant Buddhism. The last Jodo Shinshu enclave was located in Kii

Province to the south of Osaka, around the area where the castle and city of Wakayama now stand. They were called the Saiga Ikko-ikki from their location, where the strongest point was a castle called Ota. Owned by a daimyo who belonged to Jodo Shinshu, the castle had resisted an attack by Nobunaga in 1577. Not far away was the other remaining religious army in Japan: the *sohei* of Negorodera, who had very unwisely supported Tokugawa Ieyasu against Hideyoshi during the Komaki campaign of 1584. This folly brought about terrible retribution on them the following year. The result was the almost total destruction of the Negorodera complex in as thorough a job of destruction as Nobunaga had performed on Hieizan. Hideyoshi then turned his attentions towards the Saiga Ikko-ikki. Just as in Kaga a number of villages, 26 in all, had banded together for mutual defence and economic power, but when their main base at Ota was destroyed they surrendered, and thus the last armed enclave of Jodo Shinshu disappeared from Japan.

An 'aerial view' provided by the model of Torigoe and Futoge castles in the Ikko-ikki Museum, Torigoe. Futoge is at the top left. The Dainichigawa divides the two mountains from each other.

The Nishi Daimon (western great gate) at Negorodera is a gateway with no walls or gates, as befitted the peaceful times when it replaced its predecessor. The previous gateway would have been easier to fortify.

Chronology

710	Nara becomes Japan's first capital
752	Dedication of the Todaiji
794	Japan's capital is moved to Heian (Kyoto)
949	First recorded incident of violence between Japanese temples
1173	Birth of Shinran, founder of Jodo Shinshu
1180	First battle of Uji – defeat of the Miidera monks
1181	Nara receives temporary fortifications but is burned down
1221	Nara monks are involved in the Shokyu War
1321	Kakunyo converts the Otani mausoleum into the Honganji temple
1415	Birth of Rennyo Shonin, the reformer of Jodo Shinshu
1471	Rennyo founds Yoshizaki Gobo
1474	Togashi Kochiyo attacks Yoshizaki Gobo but is defeated
1478	Founding of Yamashina Mido, the Kyoto Honganji
1488	Ikko-ikki take control of Kaga Province
1496	Rennyo founds Ishiyama Honganji
1499	Death of Rennyo
1531	Civil war between branches of the Ikko-ikki in Kaga and Echizen
1532	Nichiren sect and Rokkaku Sadayori sack Yamashina Mido
1533	Shonyo makes Ishiyama Honganji the Jodo Shinshu headquarters
1536	*Sohei* from Hieizan destroy the Nichiren temples in Kyoto
1538	Shonyo negotiates the founding of a *jinaimachi* in Osaka
1546	Founding of Oyama Gobo in present-day Kanazawa
1554	Kennyo Kosa becomes the 11th *zasu* of Ishiyama Honganji
1562	Fire destroys much of the *jinaimachi* of Ishiyama Honganji
1564	Tokugawa Ieyasu defeats the Ikko-ikki of Mikawa at the battle of Azukizaka
1570	Oda Nobunaga's first attack on Ishiyama Honganji
1571	Oda Nobunaga burns Enryakuji
1573	Nobunaga's generals invade Echizen but are repulsed
1574	Oda Nobunaga destroys Nagashima
1575	Nobunaga's generals take main Ikko-ikki sites in Echizen
1576	Shibata Katsuie captures Miyukizuka (modern-day Komatsu) in Kaga
1578	Nobunaga breaks Mori's supply lines at the battle of Kizugawaguchi
1580	Surrender of Ishiyama Honganji
1581	Katsuie retakes Torigoe and Futoge
1582	Ikko-ikki recapture Torigoe and Futoge but Nobunaga then destroys them
1585	Toyotomi Hideyoshi defeats Negorodera and the Saiga Ikko-ikki
1591	Hideyoshi restores the Honganji
1602	Tokugawa Ieyasu founds Higashi Honganji, thus splitting Jodo Shinshu

Design features of the fortified temple (I): the sacred space

Unlike ordinary Buddhist temples, every fortified temple had both a sacred and a secular function to perform, and in the turbulent times of medieval Japan this effectively meant the performance of a role associated with peace and a role connected to war. The structure and design of the buildings and their layout reflect the interplay between the two roles.

We will look first at the peaceful role that a fortified temple performed. The sacred role of the buildings of any Buddhist institution, either in medieval

Two splendid *Nio* provide a spiritual guard on either side of the entrance to Daigoji, which lay in ruins for much of the 16th century after the Onin War had destroyed all its buildings except for its magnificent pagoda. Hideyoshi undertook its restoration in the final years of his life. The *Nio-mon* gate and *kondo* were transferred from Negorodera in 1598 and rededicated in 1600.

Japan or today, first consists of providing an area where the ritual demands of Buddhism may be exercised. Second, there is a need for space wherein the material needs of its clergy, such as food and living accommodation, may be met. In a monastic situation the space needed for the latter function might be quite large, but it would never detract from the primacy of the former, to which the finest architectural and decorative design would be directed. The populist nature of Jodo Shinshu added a third sacred role: that of providing adequate room for worship for a large congregation of lay people. As homes and workplaces were often provided for them within the defensive perimeter, this final function led ultimately to the creation of the *jinaimachi*.

Surviving plans and illustrations and the results of archaeological investigation of fortified temple sites show that by and large there was a total separation in architectural terms between the buildings associated with the sacred function and the other parts of the temple complex concerned with providing its defence. There were exceptions and variations to this depending on the size of the site available and its topographical layout, as we will see, but effectively we can study the layout of a Japanese fortified temple as if it were two separate units. These were the temple, laid out according to a fairly standard model depending largely on the Buddhist sect to which it owed its allegiance, and the defensive perimeter that resembled in most particulars the contemporary castles of the secular samurai warlords.

The design features of a typical Japanese Buddhist temple

Buddhism came to Japan by way of China in the middle of the 6th century AD, so it is not surprising to find that the model adopted for the general layout of the temples where the new faith was practised was based on Chinese antecedents. The architecture of Chinese Buddhist temples derived in turn from that of the Chinese palace and, by and large, the overall pattern of a Buddhist temple compound that it gave rise to persists to this day. There are numerous variations, many of which we will note specifically in relation to the examples discussed here, but certain features have stubbornly persisted over the centuries.

The usual pattern of a Buddhist temple is based on the model of a courtyard, which is entered through a formal gateway. Because this gate symbolically marks the entrance to the precincts it may not even have closing doors or walls on either side. It may also contain a pair of huge statues called *Nio*. These half-naked giants, who stand guard over the temple entrance, are derived from Hindu deities incorporated into Buddhist cosmology. One *Nio* has its mouth open, while the other's mouth is closed.

The buildings arranged within the courtyard are solidly framed wooden structures standing on masonry terraces and crowned with graceful tiled roofs. They are built round a framework of massive vertical timbers, with large cross pieces and very intricate bracketing to support upper storeys and roofs. Each vertical support usually rests on one very large stone.

The main hall within the courtyard is called the *hondo* (or sometimes the *kondo*). The *hondo* is the focus of the layout, although this may not always be immediately apparent from the overall temple layout. The *hondo* invariably has overhanging eaves protecting an outside walkway that will stretch right around the building. This walkway is reached via a flight of stairs. The interior of the *hondo* is entered at the front by some form of door. This may be a sliding or hinged wooden door or a set of doors, with additional sliding *shoji* just inside. *Shoji* are the instantly recognizable light-framed doors with translucent paper covering them. Alternatively, the doors may be hinged at the top, so that they can be lifted up and propped open.

The main image in the temple occupies a central place within the *hondo*, while around it is the space for the priests or monks to perform services, together with some provision for lay worshippers to gather. In Jodo Shinshu temples this latter area is made deliberately large. The floor will probably be of wooden planking, augmented by *tatami* (straw mats). There will be some form of barrier to divide the sanctuary of the image from the outer area.

Outside in the courtyard there may be some or all of the following features. Lanterns are always popular. A pagoda is often to be found in the temples of the older sects, but is unusual in Jodo Shinshu temples. Pagodas came to Japan with Buddhism itself. They were originally towers for housing the remains of the Buddha as relics, but were developed for other purposes such as markers for holy places. A very common feature in nearly all temples that had obvious defensive uses was the bell tower. Unlike European bell towers, a typical Japanese example is a free-standing open wooden structure from which the huge bronze bell is suspended. It is rung using an external wooden clapper. A drum tower may also be included, although these are often enclosed two-storey structures. Temples that are also monasteries are most likely to include a lecture hall together with other similar buildings concerned with the education and ordination of monks. We may find a Sutra repository, various dormitories, living quarters and a refectory. These buildings usually stand alone, but may be connected to each other using roofed wooden corridors. Further features may include a garden and a cemetery, because Buddhist funeral rites have always been very important in Japan. A final feature could be a nearby Shinto shrine associated with the temple's foundation. Shinto is the indigenous religion of Japan, and for most of Japanese history Shinto shrines and Buddhist temples have happily co-existed, with their adherents sharing their religious lives between the two.

The early aristocratic temples of Nara

The first Buddhist temples in Japan were founded in the area around Nara, the place that became Japan's first permanent capital in AD 710. The city of Nara

The bell tower of Sokusoji, a Tendai mountain temple in Mie Prefecture. This is a typical Japanese bell tower based on the design of a simple wooden frame beneath a protective roof.

The bell at Negorodera. As in all Japanese examples, the bell hangs inside the bell tower, and is rung by using a heavy wooden external clapper, which is swung by a rope.

was laid out on a grid plan in imitation of the capital of the Tang dynasty of China, from which Japan's rulers drew their inspiration.

The statesman Fujiwara Fuhito (AD 659–720) encouraged the move to Nara by founding the Buddhist Kofukuji temple and the Shinto Kasuga shrine as the spiritual guardians of the new capital. Fuhito also protected his family's position by methodically marrying off his daughters to Japanese emperors, and it was his grandson Emperor Shomu who was to provide Nara with its largest and most glorious monument: Todaiji, built to house a colossal image of Buddha. In the buildings of Todaiji and Kofukuji we see the sacred function being exercised on a grand scale that befitted the capital of Japan. In AD 752 Todaiji, which rivalled the greatest Chinese monuments, was inaugurated in the most splendid ceremony ever witnessed in Japan.

The development of esoteric mountain temples

In AD 794 Japan's capital was moved from Nara to Kyoto via the short-lived Nagaoka. Kyoto was originally known as Heian-kyo, which gave its name to the Heian Period in Japanese history. The motive behind the move was the desire of the imperial court to free itself from the stranglehold of the great Nara monasteries. As if in answer to their prayers, not only was a new site for a capital found, but no less than two Buddhist sects also arose and rapidly became associated with the new city.

Saicho (AD 762–822), known to posterity as Dengyo Daishi, founded the Tendai sect on top of Hieizan, to the north-east of Kyoto, where he had established a monastic community in his younger days. Chinese *feng shui* taught that the north-east was the direction from which evil spirits proceeded, so Hieizan was regarded as the spiritual guardian of the new capital. It was richly endowed at Nara's expense, although Saicho was to die before he could realize his dream of having Hieizan regarded as an independent institution that ordained its own monks. After his death his temple was raised to official status and given the name of Enryakuji.

The Daibutsuden (Great Buddha Hall) of Todaiji, the world's largest wooden building.

Hieizan (Mount Hiei) was home to the *sohei* of Enryakuji. This view shows Hieizan as seen from the courtyard of Miidera, a branch temple of Enryakuji much further down the mountain.

Saicho's colleague Kukai (Kobo Daishi; AD 774–835) founded the Shingon sect of Buddhism. In AD 823 Emperor Saga presented him with Toji, one of only two Buddhist temples allowed within the city precincts. In terms of physical influence, therefore, the new Heian government seemed to have succeeded in controlling Buddhism – but there was a catch. The new Buddhist sects were esoteric in their approach. Their *mikkyo* tradition stressed the active quest for enlightenment through strenuous austerities and secret rituals. Their monks would undertake arduous mountain pilgrimages and perform long mysterious rituals in their temples. As no institution was more dependent upon ritual than the imperial court the influence of Buddhism continued, even if it was exercised in more subtle ways.

In architectural terms, independence from Nara led to the diminution of Chinese styles in the design of the Heian temples and the emergence of a national style. There were also two other factors that led to the Hieizan temples looking very different from their predecessors in Nara. The first was the association with mountains. For an esoteric sect, sacred and mysterious mountains were the obvious places to build monasteries where aspiring monks could practise rituals and undergo austerities. The result was that the courtyard model of Buddhist temple seen at Nara had to be modified because of the mountainous terrain. Halls were built on different levels and joined by mountain paths through secret valleys. Enryakuji, for example, was spread out over a vast area of the summit of Hieizan, on its peaks and in its wooded valleys.

The Konponchudo of Enryakuji on Hieizan, centre of the Tendai sect.

Another difference was found in their interior layout. The *mikkyo* sects stressed gradual initiation into secret rites, so the *hondo* of *mikkyo* temples acquired a central barrier that divided the interior into an outer part for the uninitiated and an inner sanctum. At the same time, the esoteric demands of the Shingon sect in particular led to a need for a greatly enlarged priestly space where the important rituals could be performed in utmost secrecy. In some cases this led to the creation of new types of temple buildings, such as the *gomado*, a simple building where offerings using fire (the *goma* ritual) could be performed in reasonable safety. Nevertheless, anyone such as the author who has personally witnessed the fierce flames of a Shingon

The interior of the *hondo* of Shorenji in Takayama, the oldest surviving Jodo Shinshu building.

goma ritual emerges astounded that a building made of wood could ever withstand such treatment!

The Tendai and Shingon temples also took very seriously their role of serving the populace, as distinct from emphasizing the needs of the aristocracy. This requirement to be available to the laity in order to instruct and enlighten them caused further problems of space that the old Nara models could not accommodate. Pictorial evidence suggests that, like vassals in an imperial audience, any congregation in a Nara temple, even high-ranking ones, had to make do with the open air of the courtyard, with perhaps some form of temporary shelter if the weather was inclement. To cope with the conflicting demands of secrecy and education, three improvements to the plan of the *hondo* were evaluated during the Heian Period. The first was to add an aisle across the front, covered by an extension of the main roof. This is the model found in the most important Tendai building of all: the Konponchudo (Central Main Hall) of Enryakuji, founded in AD 788. The second was the provision of a building just in front of the *hondo*, either free-standing or joined to it by a gallery. This was already common in Shinto shrines, where it was known as a *raido* or a *haiden*. The third improvement, which was to become very important in Jodo Shinshu, was to construct a *raido* as the fore-hall in contact with the main building of the *hondo*, or more simply as an integral part of it under one roof. This model gave the Heian monks the best of both worlds. The laity could be accommodated with ease, while sliding partitions enabled the monks to just as easily exclude them from anything deemed improper for their eyes.

The 'peoples' temples' of Jodo Shinshu

The populist nature of sects like Jodo Shinshu inevitably led to changes in the architecture of its buildings. The first change was the shift in orientation from a south-facing *hondo* to one that looked towards the east because Amida Buddha, the focus of devotion in Jodo Shinshu, faces east from his western paradise. Other major changes arose from the fact that Jodo Shinshu temples were not monasteries but popular temples served by comparatively few priests. There were no cloistered corridors, lecture halls or pagodas. Nor do we see formal dormitory and refectory blocks. The quarters for the married priests were more like private houses, walled off from the public area in their gardens.

But the most striking difference concerned the *hondo*. First, it was likely to be dedicated not to any conventional figure in the Buddhist pantheon but to Shinran Shonin as a *goeido* (founder's hall). Second, a very common feature in the larger Jodo Shinshu establishments was the existence of two main halls instead of just one. The second hall was dedicated to Amida and was smaller, although it often had two storeys rather than one and appeared richer in detail. The *goeido* would have had a more imposing gateway, but the gate of the *amidado*, although smaller, may have had the special elaboration of an ornate roof with curved gables. The size of both halls was intended to make their *raido* spacious enough for a crowd of worshippers. The rear was closed off by a partition while the congregation assembled, but the partition was then drawn back. So, although the *raido* style was derived from esoteric Tendai worship, it served a religion in which the ceremonies were performed in public.

Design features of the fortified temple (II): the temple as a defensive system

The temporary fortifications of the *sohei*

The earlier monastic institutions of Nara and Hieizan had nothing in the way of permanent fortifications. We will therefore study their buildings in relation to the natural defensive features of the sites chosen for them and the temporary fortifications such as walls and ditches that were erected in times of war.

The two centres of *sohei* activity in early medieval Japan could not have been more different in terms of their layout and defensive capability. The temples of Nara lay in their own grounds within a fine city on a flat plain. The temples of Hieizan were hidden within mountain valleys or stood proudly upon mountain peaks. Temporary fortifications for Nara are mentioned in the *Heike Monogatari* account of Taira Shigehira's attack on Nara in 1181. We read how the monks dug ditches across the roads and erected breastworks and palisades. The breastworks would probably have been earthworks made from ditches, with the soil piled up behind to make a parapet. Fences of stakes could have been added, and they would also have made use of rows of wooden shields. These solid wooden shields, made familiar in many picture scrolls of the period, were often erected on battlefields. They had a hinged strut at the rear for support, and were often decorated at the front with the samurai leader's *mon* (family crest). Monastic armies, however, would often paint *bonji* (sacred Sanskrit ideographs) on the front of their shields.

When Miidera, which lay at the foot of Hieizan, was threatened, similar precautions were taken, and the ready supply of wood from the forests on its slope provided extra means of defence. Trees would be cut down and laid with their branches facing towards the enemy. Logs could be cut and piled, ready to roll down a path against an advancing column. However, the haughty Enryakuji on Hieizan's summit seems never to have made use of any artificial defence in all its history. Its self-confidence as the protector of Kyoto and the Alma Mater of the founders of almost every Buddhist sect in Japan gave it an arrogance and self-importance that saw no need for walls. This happy state of affairs was to be rudely shattered in September 1571 when Nobunaga's armies swept up the holy mountain, allowing no time for even a shield wall to be erected.

The defence of the early Ikko-ikki temples

It is in the design of the defences of their fortified temples that we find the best evidence that the Ikko-ikki were not just a rabble composed of ignorant peasants. Part of the secret behind their remarkable success lay in sophisticated military technology and its uses that matched any of the contemporary *daimyo*. This military prowess was illustrated by their early enthusiasm for firearms and their skills in castle-building. In this and the following section we will see how the two achievements came together.

The Ikko-ikki sites first made skilful use of their natural positions, be they a mountain (as at Torigoe), a plateau and sea cliffs (Yoshizaki), a swampy estuary (Nagashima), or a combination of all three (the mighty Ishiyama Honganji).

A strong wooden palisade is shown here in a section from the Shimabara battle screen, together with a gate that the attackers have knocked to one side. Note also the stumps of trees.

The postern gate inside the gateway of the *ni no maru* gate of Torigoe.

Upon these sites were raised walls, towers and gates that resembled a *daimyo*'s castle in every particular bar one: at the heart of the complex, instead of a keep and a mansion, lay the buildings of the Buddhist temple to which its followers owed a fanatical adherence.

Throughout their history the design of the fortified temples of the Ikko-ikki paralleled or even led the advances in defensive technology introduced by samurai. The earliest Ikko-ikki fortified temples, therefore, would have been identical to the predominantly wooden samurai castles. These were called *yamashiro* if they were located on mountains, which was very common or *hirajiro* if they were built on a flat plain. Ground preparation was crucial in both cases. For a *yamashiro* the top of the mountain would be cleared of trees and levelled. On the resulting surface there would be built quite intricate arrangements of wooden palisades, wooden towers, gateways and domestic buildings. The solid wooden walls of the palisades were pierced with arrow slits. Towers were enclosed at the top with wooden walls or portable wooden shields, and from these vantage points archers fired longbows or simply threw down stones, the only other missile weapons available before the introduction of firearms. Domestic buildings thatched with rice straw would also be built from wood and acted as quarters for the garrison as well as reception and command areas for the general, together with stables, food stores, weapon stores and the like.

By the time of the rise of the Ikko-ikki many improvements had been introduced to the *yamashiro* model. Sometimes the forest cover was stripped away almost entirely over a large area of mountain and the gaps between adjacent ridges were deepened. In such a way a roughly concentric series of mountain peaks could be converted into a number of natural inner and outer baileys, each overlooking the one below it by almost literally carving up the mountain. Ditches were strengthened by having vertical cross pieces through them, built at right angles to the inner walls. Very steep sections were made more dramatic by having long channels cut out of them, down which rocks could be rolled. Mountain streams were diverted into gullies to create moats and reservoirs, and entrances to gateways were offset to allow an enemy's approach to be covered completely.

Wooden walls were commonly of two types. The first were loose open palisades, designed to hinder an attacker's progress, slowing him down and making him an easier target for missile fire. The second type were stronger affairs built from solid wooden planking, sometimes with loopholes cut into them. These wooden palisades would often be augmented by having strong supporting timbers on their inner side along which planks could be laid to produce two levels for missile fire. Trees were planted in castles to bind the soil and also to shield the castle from view, but too many trees in a castle's bailey could be inconvenient in a siege situation and would be cut down before an attack.

Temple defences in the age of gunpowder

Around the middle of the 16th century some very important developments took place in Japanese fortress technology. Castles were growing larger to accommodate the increasing numbers of troops a samurai commander now employed. A wider area allowed more elaborate walls and buildings to be raised, and in place of the loose wooden palisades of the old days stronger walls could be built using a form of wattle and daub construction. Stout vertical wooden posts were driven into the earth at six-foot intervals with bamboo poles placed between them and bundles of bamboo, lashed together with rope, as the core. The resulting structures were plastered with a mixture of red clay and crushed rock, and were often whitewashed, giving a Japanese castle its characteristic appearance. Arrow ports were cut at regular intervals. To keep weather damage to a minimum the walls were topped with sloping thatch, wooden shingles, or even tiles.

But expansion of a site caused its own problems on a restricted and uneven mountain top. To bind the soil on exposed sections grass was allowed to grow,

A detail from the screen in Osaka Castle depicting the battle of Shizugatake in 1583, showing a typical stone castle base topped by plaster walls. There are two sorts of loophole: square ones for bows, round ones for arquebuses, from which the barrels of the guns protrude. Portable wooden shields of a type used for centuries in Japan provide extra defence.

but the torrential rain experienced in Japan took a heavy toll of foundations and structures alike. Even if there were no typhoons, earthquakes or sieges to create additional havoc, normal wear and tear demanded that the plastered walls be routinely repaired at least every five years. If stronger, and therefore heavier, structures were to be added, something more substantial than a grassy bank was needed as a castle base, and the solution to this problem was to provide the Japanese castle with its most enduring visual features. These were the great stone bases, a fundamental design element also to be found in the fortified temples. The stone bases consisted of an earthen core, often, but not always, carved out of the mountainside, that was faced with huge stones arranged in a precise mathematical curve that maximized the strength and allowed for the shock of earthquakes. Such was their strength that the one at Hiroshima withstood the atomic bomb blast in 1945, though the entire wooden superstructure was blown away. These strong bases allowed the development of the tower keeps of Japanese castles, a feature replaced in the fortified temple by the sacred buildings.

The major military innovation of the times was the introduction of firearms. Guns, of which the prototypes came originally from Portugal, were first used in battle in Japan in 1549. They were hand-held matchlock muskets or arquebuses, fired by dropping a smouldering match on to a touchhole. Larger-calibre guns existed, but siege cannon as understood by Western Europe did not really appear until the siege of Osaka in 1614/15. Instead the most common technique that developed in a siege situation was mass controlled volley firing that could clear the walls of a castle or temple of its attackers. The Ikko-ikki and the Negorodera monks were among the first to appreciate the use of gunpowder weapons, and one of the earliest examples of volley firing in the defence of a castle occurred when Oda Nobunaga was driven away from the Ishiyama Honganji during his first attack on it in 1570. All subsequent operations involving the Ikko-ikki involved considerable use of firearms on both sides, so how did this affect the appearance of their fortress temples?

The reconstruction of Ishiyama Honganji, discussed in detail below, strongly suggests that the Ikko-ikki designed their later fortified temples in a way that allowed clear fields of defensive fire with a minimum of blind spots. The result, when resources and topography allowed it, was a series of stone walls topped by low plaster walls that interlocked and covered each other like a Japanese folding screen. From loopholes in the plastered sections hundreds, even thousands, of arquebuses could be brought to bear. Such defences are illustrated on the screen in Osaka Castle depicting the battle of Shizugatake in 1583. This was the battle from which Maeda Toshiie went on to capture the Ikko-ikki fortified temple of Oyama Gobo in Kanazawa, so we may envisage the defences of the latter place as being not unlike the wall shown on the screen. We see the typical stone base topped by plaster walls. There are two sorts of loophole: square ones for bows; round ones for arquebuses, from which the barrels of the guns protrude. The portable wooden shields, of a type used for centuries in Japan, provide extra defence.

The final innovation that can be credited to the Ikko-ikki lies in their creation of *jinaimachi*. From the outset the *jinaimachi* were seen as an integral part of the fortified temple's community, and therefore played a role in its defence. The outer defensive perimeter would be located around the *jinaimachi*, which itself was located in a defensible space. Thus rivers and other natural features were used. Natural slopes, rivers and streams, forests and bamboo groves provided cover and defence, while the design of the streets of the *jinaimachi* was always a deliberately complex one intended to mislead the attackers.

Representative fortified temples of Japan

In this section I shall describe key sites of the *sohei* and *monto* as they were in their heyday. Some no longer exist, whilst others were destroyed and rebuilt several times over and are reconstructed on the basis of literary, pictorial and archaeological evidence.

The *sohei* temples of Nara

Kofukuji, the centre of the Hosso sect of Buddhism, was begun in AD 710 and completed by about AD 730. It was assigned a four-block square in Nara's

Details of the inner defences of a gateway, showing locking bars. This is the outer gate of the Koshoji of Tondabayashi. The gate is believed to have been transferred from Hideyoshi's Fushimi Castle.

The five-storey pagoda of Kofukuji, built in AD 725 and restored in 1426. The multi-storey wooden pagodas of Japan are architectural wonders. It has also been discovered that the ancient wooden pagodas of Nara are the most earthquake-resistant buildings in Japan. This is because their core is a long vertical mast which, sunk into the ground, absorbs the shock.

gridiron pattern, within which the main buildings stood inside a rectangle one block wide by two blocks deep. At the time of the warrior monks the *hondo* arose from the centre of this area and gave the impression of great size. It was nine bays across by six bays deep, 41 by 26m. There were also two lesser halls known as *kondo* (golden halls). Kofukuji boasted just one pagoda, the magnificent five-storey structure that stands to this day.

The area allotted to the Todaiji, eight city blocks on each side, was four times the area of Kofukuji and equalled that of the imperial palace precincts. All of its elements were built on the same impressive scale. The Nandaimon (Great Southern Gate) was a masterpiece of its kind, with huge *Nio* in the niches. The compound had two pagodas, each seven storeys tall and some 108m to the tip of each spire. The Daibutsuden (Great Buddha Hall) was a colossal wooden structure of 11 bays by seven, half as large again as its present replacement, which is the largest wooden building in the world. The temples of Nara had no military involvement in the whole of the *Sengoku Jidai*, so any further changes to the designs arose from calamities such as fires and earthquakes.

The fortified temple in the age prior to gunpowder: Yoshizaki Gobo, 1474

The fortified temple in the age prior to gunpowder: Yoshizaki Gobo, 1474

Yoshizaki Gobo, founded by Rennyo when he fled from the *sohei* (warrior monks) of Hieizan in 1471, was Japan's first permanently fortified temple. It was built to resist attacks by bows and arrows, fire and edged weapons, and is shown as it would have appeared when it came under attack by Togashi Kochiyo in 1474. This reconstruction is based on a model on display in the Rennyo Kinenkan in Yoshizaki, which was constructed using details in a contemporary scroll painting in the possession of Yoshizakiji and information from archaeological investigation.

Lake Kitagana as seen from the Chitoseyama plateau, the site of Yoshizaki Gobo. The island of Shikajima covers the waterway leading to the sea. The defensive possibilities that impressed Rennyo are quite apparent.

Yoshizaki Gobo – the first permanently fortified temple

Yoshizaki Gobo, which lies on the historic border between Echizen Province and Kaga Province, was founded by Rennyo in 1471 after he had fled from Kyoto. The land on which Yoshizaki Gobo was to be built was owned by the samurai Oei Yoshihisa, the local village head. A convert to Jodo Shinshu, he donated a parcel of land to Rennyo that included Chitoseyama (Mount Chitose). While the temple was being constructed Rennyo lived in his benefactor's house, the site of which is now occupied by Yoshizakiji. In 1474 the patron performed a further valuable service to Jodo Shinshu when he rescued Rennyo from a fire, carrying the older man to safety on his back.

In a letter of 1473 Rennyo wrote that he had selected the site of Yoshizaki Gobo on account of its scenic beauty, but that was only part of the story. Chitoseyama, the focal point of the site, had obvious defensive possibilities, being the highest point on a peninsula that projected into Lake Kitagana. The lake was connected to the sea by a narrow waterway protected at its exit from the lake by a small forested island called Shikajima.

Our sources for the reconstruction of Yoshizaki Gobo are a contemporary scroll painting displayed in the Yoshizakiji Museum, a woodblock drawing of 1847 and archaeological investigations. The plateau of Chitoseyama covered 33,000m^2, and was surrounded on all sides by cliffs. There was a path on the eastern side leading down to an area of flat land on the northern side, the only such path on the whole site, where boats could be launched into the lake. The southern side was also defended by cliffs, leaving only a narrow neck of vulnerable land at the extreme eastern side.

A hanging scroll showing Yoshizaki Gobo, displayed in the Yoshizakiji Museum in Yoshizaki. The Amida hall is the simpler structure with an open-roofed area. The *goeido* is fronted by a gateway. In the case of Yoshizaki Gobo, these buildings have been joined by a third, smaller structure on the rear (western) side, presumably to provide private accommodation for Rennyo himself.

29

The buildings of Yoshizaki Gobo on the plateau have long since disappeared and have never been replaced. Land has been reclaimed from the lakeside, and this is where the modern village is located.

The plateau of Chitoseyama was the location of the temple buildings. Taking the scroll painting as a guide, we recognize the common feature of a *goeido* and *amidado* connected by a covered walkway. The Amida hall is the simpler structure with an open-roofed area. The *goeido* is fronted by a gateway. In the case of Yoshizaki Gobo, these buildings have been joined by a third, smaller structure on the rear (western) side, presumably to provide private accommodation for Rennyo himself. The only other structure within the courtyard is a smaller building that was probably a bell tower. A low temple wall divides the courtyard area from other buildings outside on the southern side.

From this cluster of buildings a winding hairpin path led down to the lake on the western side of the plateau, while a gentler path led around the slope to descend on the eastern side amongst more buildings. A steeper descent could be made by means of two flights of stone stairs on the vulnerable, but steep, eastern side. The side was defended by sloping stone walls identical in design to those commonly found in Japanese castles. The walls overlooked the flat lakeside area. Beyond the landing stages and beach were more houses, rice fields and narrow paths that made up Yoshizaki's *jinaimachi*. They were surrounded on the lake fringes by dense woods. We know from Rennyo's own statement that during the two years after his arrival, well over 200 separate residences were built to accommodate the flow of pilgrims attracted to the site by its famous newcomer.

Nagashima – defence of river and sea

The Ikko-ikki base at Nagashima is the easiest to envisage in outline and the most difficult to reconstruct in detail. The overall picture presented by descriptions of Nagashima is of a community located on a vast, remote and lonely river delta where three great wide rivers, the Kiso, Nagara and Ina, enter the sea. There was no high ground for miles, and its inhabitants were clustered on to a series of islands amid sea, river and marsh, with numerous creeks and inlets. Sandbanks shifted as the years went by. Islands disappeared or were saved as *waju* (dyked communities), while the whole area was regularly battered by typhoons and high tides. Little was visible from sea level because of the maze of reed beds, whose dense fronds waved in the wind, now and then blowing to one side to reveal simple wooden palisades concealing simple wooden buildings. Here and there the roof of a higher building, perhaps a temple, protruded above the monotonous landscape, while tall wooden watchtowers gave the only indication from a distance that this was a military establishment.

This was the environment from which the Ikko-ikki of Nagashima defied Oda Nobunaga for several desperate years until his combination of naval control and the deadly weapon of fire stripped Nagashima of its defences. The wooden walls of Nagashima were augmented by other unique defensive devices when danger threatened. The shores of the reed beds were booby-trapped by the simple addition of old pots and vases buried up to the necks in the sand to provide a trap for ankles. Ropes tied on to stakes just below the water level were the contemporary equivalent of tripwires.

The combination of a constantly changing river landscape buffeted by typhoons and transformed in modern times by drainage programmes has removed from Nagashima any trace of its occupation by the Ikko-ikki. The

The Ikko-ikki base at Nagashima was completely destroyed by Oda Nobunaga in 1574, but Takigawa Kazumasu built a castle there after the Ikko-ikki had gone. It appears on this Edo Period painted screen in Komaki Castle as a classic Japanese castle surrounded by absolutely nothing. To the north of the island on which the castle is built are shown empty islands fringed with reeds.

only reconstruction possible therefore comes from one's imagination. The heart of the religious community was a fortified temple called Ganshoji, which has since been rebuilt and provides an excellent illustration of a straightforward Jodo Shinshu temple. Its position among acres of flat rice fields reclaimed from the sea allows it to dominate the landscape in a way that few other temples of that size can do.

Torigoe – temple as *yamashiro*

Reference was made earlier to the strong resemblance between the defensive elements of a fortified temple and the contemporary samurai castle. This is no coincidence, because many of the prime movers within the Jodo Shinshu sect and its Ikko-ikki armies were samurai. Like their secular counterparts the Ikko-ikki commanders faced the same challenges posed by contemporary fortress technology and the strict rigours of the Japanese landscape.

Nowhere is the solution to these problems better seen in the fortified temple context than at Torigoe, the archetypal temple/castle. It is the only temple/castle site to have been comprehensively excavated. The published results, the findings displayed in the nearby Ikko-ikki Museum (the only one of its kind) and some sensitive on-site restorations provide much valuable information about the last important Ikko-ikki *yamashiro*.

Torigoe is located in the southern part of modern Ishikawa Prefecture, the old province of Kaga, about 19km from the city

Torigoe, where a fortified temple is almost indistinguishable from a samurai's castle.

of Komatsu. It lies on the top of a 312m-high mountain overlooking the Tedorigawa (Tedori River) at a strategic point where it is joined by the Dainichigawa. Together with its sister fortress of Futoge across the valley at the slightly lower elevation of 286m, the site of Torigoe dominates the area, and in 1582 it was to provide a suitably dramatic location for the last stand of the Kaga Ikko-ikki.

Excavation of Torigoe was carried out between 1977 and 1995 and has yielded very valuable results that allow us to appreciate the nature of an Ikko-ikki *yamashiro*. The Jodo Shinshu temple, the heart of the community, would have been

The view from the summit of the mountain on which Torigoe stands, showing how the fortress temple dominated the landscape. The modern Ikko-ikki Museum may be seen beside the road.

The fortified temple as *yamashiro*:
Torigoe, 1582

The fortified temple as *yamashiro*: Torigoe, 1582

This plate shows the *hon maru* (innermost bailey) and *ni no maru* (second bailey) of Torigoe as they would have appeared prior to Oda Nobunaga's final assault in 1582. It is a typical small, isolated, fortified temple that appears to float in the morning mist in the valley below. The fortifications have been reconstructed based on archaeological evidence and the reconstructed buildings on site, some of which make use of the limited stone that was available. The religious buildings within the *hon maru* are based on existing contemporary structures elsewhere, particularly Shorenji at Takayama, built in 1504.

located within the wooden walls of the highest and innermost of three irregularly shaped baileys: the *san no maru* (third bailey), the *ni no maru* (second bailey) and the *hon maru* (innermost bailey). Each was built on slightly higher ground that the preceding level, in keeping with the Japanese practice of levelling a mountain top to give good defensive space. The complete defensive area covered about 2,000m², almost one-sixteenth the size of the Yoshizaki Gobo.

The reconstruction of small sections of various military structures allows us to envisage the castle as a whole, although unfortunately no reconstruction has been carried out for the religious buildings. The appearance of these may however be inferred from the archaeological findings (mainly post holes) and by comparison with other similar buildings elsewhere. When the dig commenced numerous post holes were discovered. These would have held the large single-stone foundations on which each upright wooden pillar of the temple buildings was individually supported. The *hon maru* was a near perfect rectangle that narrowed slightly towards the rear because of the presence at the front of the enclosure of a watchtower. It measured approximately 50m by 21m. A layer of black ash was found from the time of the castle's final fall and subsequent destruction.

The archaeologists concluded that at the time of the sieges of 1581–82 there were three buildings within the *hon maru* courtyard. The largest building, probably a *goeido*, covered an area covered by seven post holes by six, thus giving the building an approximate floor size of 15m by 10m deep. The post holes make a perfect rectangle, indicating that the *goeido* was a simple building without any projecting porch. It would therefore seem reasonable to assume that the *goeido* was very similar in appearance to the contemporary Shorenji in Takayama.

The other two buildings within the *hon maru* were probably the living quarters for the garrison or had other military purposes. One is directly in front of the entrance, suggesting a role as a guardhouse when the location of the *goeido* was planned. Also within the *hon maru* is the castle well, now surrounded by a low wooden fence. Preparations for a siege may be seen in the large earthenware storage jars sunk into the ground of the *hon maru*. Two of the jars are on show in the Ikko-ikki Museum.

The *hon maru* was enclosed by an inner wooden palisade, reconstructed on site as an open fence of sharpened stakes. There is also an earthen wall. The key to the defences of the *hon maru* was the corner tower and the gateway. The gatehouse is offset from the centre of the wall and is a simple two-storey affair of square plan using four large-diameter timbers as the vertical supports. The solid wooden gates swing back on hinges underneath the guard tower that is open at the rear, but which has narrow window slits at the front. There is a low balustrade running round it, and the whole has a sloping wooden roof. A wooden palisade

The well of Torigoe. In the background is the gate of the *hon maru* and markers showing the post holes of a building. Note the reconstructed fences and gates as described in the text.

The gateway and *koguchi* (barbican) that defend the perimeter of the *hon maru* at Torigoe.

The view today from the keep of Osaka Castle, the site of Ishiyama Honganji.

stretches out on either side of the gate to join the earthwork in a staggered fashion. The outline of the base of the corner tower is indicated on the ground, and would probably have been the simple three- or four-storey version found in many contemporary castles, enclosed at the top in a fashion similar to the gateway.

The ground drops away sharply from the *hon maru*, where there is an extra line of defence in the form of a quite sophisticated dressed-stone *koguchi* (barbican). At Futoge Castle across the valley there is a square *koguchi*. Seen from above the Torigoe *koguchi* has the appearance of a small conventional castle wall with sloping outer surfaces. The *koguchi* has a gateway, again offset, requiring attackers to turn to the right before entering the *hon maru*. This gate is of a different design from the *hon maru* gate. It is one storey high and has no guardroom above it, but the gates swing open under the shelter of two small roofs.

Beyond the *koguchi* we are in the *ni no maru*, the defensive perimeter of which consists of a planking fence with firing places above a ditch that continues down to the natural slope of the mountain. It also extends around the edge of the *ni no maru* to face back on itself against the *hon maru* area. Thus cover could be provided against any attackers ascending the slope between the hon maru and the *ni no maru*.

The reconstructed *ni no maru* fence is pierced by two very simple gateways consisting of two uprights but no gate. However, at the point where the *ni no maru* is left to begin the long journey down a steep mountain top, we find what are effectively the outer defences of the 'citadel'. A low earth mound around the site provided cover, while the path is individually guarded by a very solid gate. It is very similar to the *hon maru* gate but is stronger with an enclosed gatehouse and a small postern gate to its side. There is no balustrade around the outside, but once again the solid fence is integrated with the earth mound.

Ishiyama Honganji – the fortified cathedral

Ishiyama Honganji was the headquarters of the Ikko-ikki for most of the time the organization was involved in war. It was the largest establishment within Jodo Shinshu, lasted a full century, and presented an amalgam of defensive features that enabled it to withstand Oda Nobunaga for an entire decade.

Not a single trace of Ishiyama Honganji's walls or buildings remains to this day. The one general fact known about it is that it occupied the site now filled by Osaka Castle. The precincts of Osaka Castle today are a welcome expanse of grass and water within the modern city with its gleaming skyscrapers, but because of this it is very difficult to appreciate that Rennyo's hermitage for his retirement was built upon a 'long slope'. Yet this is what lies under 21st-century Osaka: a long slope leading up to the Uemachi plateau.

By the time Rennyo moved to Osaka the place already had a long history of settlement. Known first as Naniwa, it had been the site of one of Japan's transient capital cities before Nara was made the permanent capital in AD 710. Naniwa was built along the Uemachi plateau and offered a convenient port in the inner recesses of a bay fed by a major river, the Yodogawa. Recent archaeological discoveries have established that Rennyo founded Ishiyama Honganji on the site of

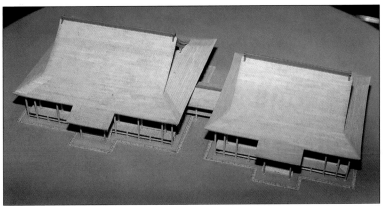

A model of the *goeido* and the *amidado* of Ishiyama Honganji in the Osaka Castle Museum.

the old imperial palace of Naniwa. The overall area was probably about 4km from the beginning of the slope at the south to the edge of the plateau where it overlooked the estuary to the north. The natural edge to the plateau provided good defence on the northern side, and would have been progressively strengthened as it levelled out. It also had its own defended harbour where the north-western quarter of the plateau sloped down to the estuary. But the Uemachi plateau was only part of Ishiyama Honganji's outer defence system, because this high ground, the only elevation for miles around, lay at the heart of a landscape similar to that of Nagashima, although it was much more developed. There were plenty of reed-covered islands, creeks, rivers, forests and rice fields to confuse any enemy who chose unwisely to leave the well-trodden road north to Kyoto or east to Nara, or to abandon the well-navigated Yodogawa and the busy navigation at the entrance of the Inland Sea.

The map, referred to in the text, showing the positions of the attacking and defending forces during the siege of Ishiyama Honganji.

Except perhaps for the steeper northern side, the original 15th-century Ishiyama Honganji would have been defended by an additional earthen embankment behind an excavated ditch. A wooden palisade of some sort would have topped the embankment, and the defences on the flat southern side would have been made the strongest. The Jodo Shinshu temple would have been located at the centre of the plateau with earthwork walls and gates of its own. No extra water defences were provided beyond those already supplied by nature. The *jinaimachi* grew within the outer walls.

Several attempts have been made in recent years to reconstruct the appearance of Ishiyama Honganji's innermost citadel. As a great deal of speculation is involved there is some variation in the conclusions drawn, but on three points there is broad agreement:

1. Ishiyama Honganji began as a simple stockade fortress but evolved in size and design over the century of its existence in a way that reflected the development of Japanese castles in general.

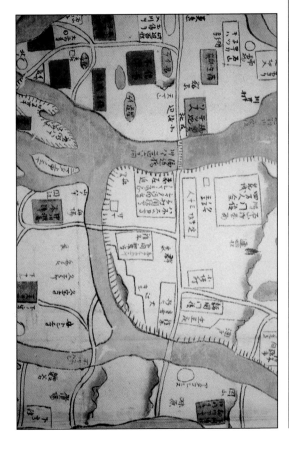

2. By the time it was attacked by Oda Nobunaga's army the Jodo Shinshu temple at Ishiyama Honganji's heart lay within concentric baileys as strong as any contemporary castle. It had sloping stone walls, plastered parapet walls, gatehouses and corner towers that would have presented the exact appearance from the outside of a strong *daimyo*'s castle.

3. The main buildings of the Jodo Shinshu temple consisted of a *goeido* and an *amidado* that were linked by a covered corridor.

The most important source for information on the appearance of the final Ishiyama Honganji in the 1570s is a contemporary map showing the disposition of the rival forces at the time of the final siege. The waterways, ponds, roads and bridges are clearly marked, and there are also some intriguing clues as to the buildings. The accompanying photograph is of one small section of the map depicting most of the island on which the fortress of Ishiyama Honganji stood. There are bridges in all directions except to the east (at the right of the photograph), while the intersections of the roads are deliberately offset to hinder attackers. The hatched marks around the side probably indicate palisades, while the shading is to show the elevated plateau. The black zigzag in the south-western corner probably represents a wall, arranged in this pattern to give covering fire. The white rectangles contain the names of the commanders of the *monto* units; red triangles on all the neighbouring islands represent the besieging armies, and the largest one to the north is labelled ominously 'Nobunaga's headquarters'.

In 1987 this map was used to build a model of the fortress area that is now on show in Namba Betsuin, a Jodo Shinshu temple in Osaka. This model has provided the basis for the accompanying plate that shows Ishiyama Honganji as it was at the time of Oda Nobunaga. The builder of the model in the Namba Betsuin subdivided the central island on the map into a number of smaller islands that were created using moats. This is a perfectly reasonable conclusion to draw in view of the ease with which this could be done and the pattern of moats used later when Hideyoshi built Osaka Castle on the site. The original 15th-century layout of Ishiyama Honganji, whereby it simply filled the space available on the Uemachi plateau with minor additions, had by this time disappeared, and a fortress that heralded the future Osaka Castle had emerged in its place. Now that moats and walls had been constructed the sloping plateau was much less discernible.

The structures of Ishiyama Honganji look increasingly formidable the nearer one moves to its religious centre. The outer moats that divide the inner fortress complex from the rest of the jinaimachi and the rice fields beyond have a natural curve, and the stone walls on either side of them are comparatively modest. The bridges are simple, and the palisades are of open-work construction with similar-looking gateways. The watchtowers are of single timbers with a flat platform at the top and would be used for fire-watching in the *jinaimachi* as well as in case of attack. But when one crosses from the network of outer islands formed by these moats and natural streams the picture changes. The well-defined inner moat, which encloses only the main temple area, frames a view that matches any samurai castle in both strength and appearance. The stone walls are high and intersect at precise angles. Along their top runs a plastered white wall protected from the weather by tiles. It is pierced by loopholes, and trees are planted along its length to shield the castle from prying eyes. Two-storey towers that look like miniature keeps stand at its four corners. There is an additional single-storey tower guarding the main east gate. The bridges across the inner moat are sturdy and supported on piers, each one terminating in a steep flight of steps that leads up to a fortified gatehouse with massive reinforced wooden doors. The progress of an attacker approaching these gates would be covered every inch of the way.

A model of the streets of Osaka as they would have appeared under Toyotomi Hideyoshi. The *jinaimachi* 20 years earlier cannot have looked very different. We see narrow streets in quarters divided from one another by gates and fences within an overall local perimeter of ditches and earthworks. Between the road and the fence is a drainage ditch.

On entering the gatehouse a visitor would find himself in the large temple courtyard covered in gravel with stone pathways linking the buildings. There is a bell tower and a drum tower, together with numerous other temple buildings that lie behind an additional low inner wall. If our visitor enters by the eastern gateway he has the finest view, which is of the *goeido* hall linked to the *amidado* by a covered corridor. Each is an imposing structure with large overhanging eaves and a covered staircase in front of the main doors of each. (The *goeido* of Ishiyama Honganji is the subject of the scale model in the new Osaka City Museum of History across the road from Osaka Castle.) The gables are carved ornately with designs of peonies and a *komainu* (mythological Chinese dog), and the scale of the *raido* is very noticeable.

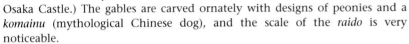

Another view of the Osaka model. The buildings are simple one-storey houses, shops and craftsmen's establishments with shingled roofs. A framework of bamboo across the surface of the sloping roofs is held down by heavy stones to stop the panels blowing away. There are gardens and wells to the rear of the buildings.

The *jinaimachi* of Ishiyama Honganji was an integral part of the settlement, and an indication of the number of dwellings within it is provided by documents relating to the rebuilding of the area after a fire in 1562. The conflagration, it was noted, had consumed 2,000 homes, while another fire destroyed 900 residences and some temple buildings in 1564. For its reconstruction we have the evidence of woodblock prints made many years later and numerous comparisons from other medieval towns. One print shows the edge of the *jinaimachi* where it meets the moat leading up to the temple buildings. The street here is wide, but the quarter that begins at its entrance gate has narrow streets and tightly packed buildings. There are shops with bright divided curtains hanging in front, as well as gardens and trees.

This is the image presented by another exhibit in the Osaka Museum of History. It is a model of the streets of Osaka as they would have appeared under Toyotomi Hideyoshi, and the *jinaimachi* 20 years earlier cannot have looked very different. We see narrow streets in quarters divided from one another by gates and fences within an overall local perimeter of ditches and earthworks. Between the road and the fence is a drainage ditch. The buildings are simple one-storey houses, shops and craftsmen's establishments with shingled roofs. A framework of bamboo across the surface of the sloping roofs is held down by heavy stones to stop the panels blowing away. There are gardens and wells to the rear of the buildings.

The *jinaimachi* of Tondabayashi

Less than an hour's train journey from the site of Ishiyama Honganji brings us to a place that was once known simply by the name of *jinaimachi* and which still evokes the spirit of the temple town. It is known today as Tondabayashi and was one of the temple towns that negotiated terms for its inhabitants that were similar to those of Ishiyama Honganji. Although none of the buildings in it date from before the Edo Period, it is worth studying for the light it shines on the idea of the *jinaimachi*. It was founded around the site of Koshoji, a Jodo Shinshu establishment dating from about 1570. The foundation was originally part of the Yamashina Mido complex, destroyed in 1532. Determined to build the new temple, the priest Shoshu acquired a patch of uncultivated grassland on top of the Ishikawa River terrace. He requested eight *shoya* (village headmen), two each from four neighbouring villages, to co-operate with him in the building of the temple, the cultivation of the fields and the construction of a town.

Apart from Koshoji no other local building has a direct connection with the Ikko-ikki, but Tondabayashi is also interesting because of its defensive location.

The fortified temple and its *jinaimachi*: Ishiyama
Honganji, 1580

The fortified temple and its *jinaimachi*: Ishiyama Honganji, 1580

The great fortified cathedral of Ishiyama Honganji and its attached *jinaimachi* (temple town) are shown here in their final developed form prior to their destruction by Oda Nobunaga in 1580. There is the usual pair of temple halls typical of Jodo Shinshu, while the defences of the site match those of a contemporary castle, particularly through the inclusion of massive stone bases. This reconstruction is based on a scale model of Ishiyama Honganji in Namba Betsuin, Osaka.

A painting of the Edo Period depicting the *jinaimachi* of Tondabayashi beside the Ishikawa River. We see a bridge across the river, and the natural defences provided by trees and water.

An illustration from *Kawachi Meisho Zukai* (collection of beautiful places in Kawachi Province), reproduced here, shows Koshoji dominating the town. Fences and foliage, particularly bamboo groves, protect it to the river's edge, where a series of very rudimentary bridges link it to the area across the river. For security purposes, visibility at intersections of roads was reduced by specially designing them so that they did not cross at right angles.

The original *kondo* of Negorodera, now at Daigoji near Kyoto. It was first built early in the Kamakura Period (1185–1392) in the developing national style. It is an excellent example of an early temple hall, and contains a main image of Yakushi Nyorai which is probably contemporary with the building. The survival of the *kondo* and the images is quite remarkable given Hideyoshi's fire attack on Negorodera in 1585.

Negorodera – the fortress of the last of the *sohei*

Negorodera provides a unique example of a warrior monk temple of the Shingon sect. Unlike the other temples mentioned in this book, its name is pronounced using the Japanese reading of the characters rather than the Chinese style, so the suffix for 'temple' is read as '-dera' rather than '-ji'. It is possible to reconstruct its appearance in about 1585 with a high likelihood of accuracy for two reasons. First, the site still exists in the same location and is still a Shingon temple. Second, several of the original buildings have survived. Only three of the buildings remain on the site itself, but the removal by Hideyoshi of the others to the Shingon temple of Daigoji near Kyoto has ensured their survival. There are also a considerable number of pictorial illustrations of Negorodera monks. This is largely because they were finally quelled by Toyotomi Hideyoshi, whose illustrated biographies furnish us with some fascinating details of the physical appearance of the last of the *sohei*.

Negorodera owes its fame to the Buddhist priest Kakuban (1095–1143), known to posterity as Kogyo Daishi. He was regarded by his followers as a reformer and restorer of Shingon, much in the same way as Rennyo was viewed within Jodo Shinshu. Kogyo Daishi was given the estate containing Negorodera by former Emperor Go Toba in 1132, and grew to exercise great influence within Shingon. His views met with opposition from rivals on Koyasan, so that he was eventually driven out and retired to Negorodera. Kogyo Daishi's faction became known as the Shingi (which translates as 'new meaning') branch of the Shingon sect, but there was never the tragic split that other sects were to experience. Instead the monks of Negorodera channelled their energies against samurai. Just like the Ikko-ikki they were early converts to firearm technology, largely through the influence of the priest Suginobo Myosan. He was the brother of a certain Tsuda Katsunaga, who happened to visit the territories of the Shimazu *daimyo* in 1543, the same year that the Portuguese first arrived in Japan. Katsunaga was given an arquebus as a gift. Suginobo took it back to Negorodera, where a local smith copied it and began producing guns for the Negorodera *sohei*.

The Negorodera complex was built in a naturally strong position on the southern slopes of the Katsuragi mountains, the dense forested peaks of which protected it from the north. The site also made clever use of a number of minor rivers that flowed down from the mountains to divide sections of the Negorodera from each other. The Otanigawa, Bodaigawa and Rengeda-Tnigawa merged into the Negorogawa having already created three moats for the fortified temple. To the west of the Rengedanigawa were two small lakes or large ponds, the Ote ike and the Shin ike, while a much larger lake lay further to the west again. The modern road follows the southern boundary of the temple north of the lower rivers. Here, where the ground still sloped away, were Negorodera's southern defences. A steep decline was left forested except where the area was cleared immediately in front of gates and strongpoints to provide a clear field of fire. The artificial defence here was an earthen embankment topped by a palisade.

Negorodera's loveliest architectural treasure: the Daito or Great Pagoda. It was built in 1496 and is of a form known as the *tahoto* ('pagoda of many treasures'). Bullet holes from 1585 are the only embellishment to Negorodera's perfect specimen.

The gateway to the Aizen-In at Negorodera. The Aizen-In was the residence of Suginobo Myosan, who was largely responsible for introducing firearms to the Negorodera army.

Along its length were simple towers and one gateway from which a path dropped away steeply. An open wooden watchtower was established at the western end. Behind the embankment were more trees; then came the natural moat of the Negorogawa and Bodaigawa. The actual temple compound lay just inside this line and was protected by a ditch and long plaster walls of modest height. On the steepest slopes were artificial gullies down which rocks could be rolled.

A comparison between the layout of Negorodera and Ishiyama Honganji illustrates the difference between a Shingon establishment and a Jodo Shinshu temple on one hand, and the constraints

The interior of the *kondo* (main hall) of Daigoji near Kyoto. This was originally the main hall of Negorodera, and was moved to its present location after Hideyoshi's attack in 1585. It is an excellent example of the simple interior décor of a Shingon temple in the Kamakura Period (1185–1392). The central image is of Yakushi Nyorai, the Buddha of healing.

on building forced by the two very different locations of a wooded mountain and a swampy estuary on the other. The buildings of Negorodera extended over a vast area, and consist of a number of different compounds. The sheer extent of Negorodera was one reason why Hideyoshi's capture of it in 1585, which made much use of fire, did not destroy the whole compound but allowed Hideyoshi to salvage some choice pieces of architecture as loot. The mountain streams that acted as moats would also have been useful firebreaks.

The temple halls also have particular functions, as noted earlier, for the esoteric rituals of the Shingon sect, and much of the original layout survives to this day as separate compounds and courtyards. In the south-western corner, near to the Ote pond, was the Aizen-In, the residence of the monk Suginobo Myosan, who was largely responsible for the development of firearms. Its single-storey gatehouse still exists. Nearby is a very fine temple gateway, the Nishi Daimon (western great gate) that was the main entrance to the Negorodera from the west. The present structure is a replacement for the original, which is believed to have become the main gate at Daigoji.

In the centre of the complex lie a number of buildings dating from the Edo Period that replace others lost in the fire. One, the Honbo, the residence of the chief priest, includes beautiful Edo Period gardens. Similar gardens may well have been a feature of the original Negorodera. On the eastern extremity of the site the deity Fudo is the focus of attention, worshipped inside an octagonal Fudodo.

Further up the mountain on the eastern side lies Negorodera's most important courtyard. It reaches to the mountain itself, and was spared the fire of 1585. Here is found Negorodera's loveliest architectural treasure: the Daito or Great Pagoda. It was built in 1496 and is of a form known as the *tahoto* ('pagoda of many treasures'). The style is associated particularly with the Tendai and Shingon sects, and is a variation on the Indian stupa, as transformed by Chinese culture. In China the cylindrical body of the stupa with its domed top was modified by giving it a roof. In Japan the dome was of plaster over a wooden framework, so to protect it from the weather the *tahoto* acquired an extra roof, thus providing its final appearance. Bullet holes from 1585 are the only embellishment to Negorodera's perfect specimen.

Next to the pagoda lies another building to have escaped Hideyoshi's fire: the Daishido, a small hall that encloses an image of Kobo Daishi, the founder of the Shingon sect. To its rear is Negoroji's *kondo*, built in 1801 to replace the original building that was moved to Daigoji after Hideyoshi's attack. The first *kondo*, now perfectly preserved, was constructed during the Kamakura Period (1185–1392). The central image inside is of Yakushi Nyorai, the Buddha of healing.

A bamboo grove provides a natural defence for Tondabayashi on the slope leading down to the Ishikawa River.

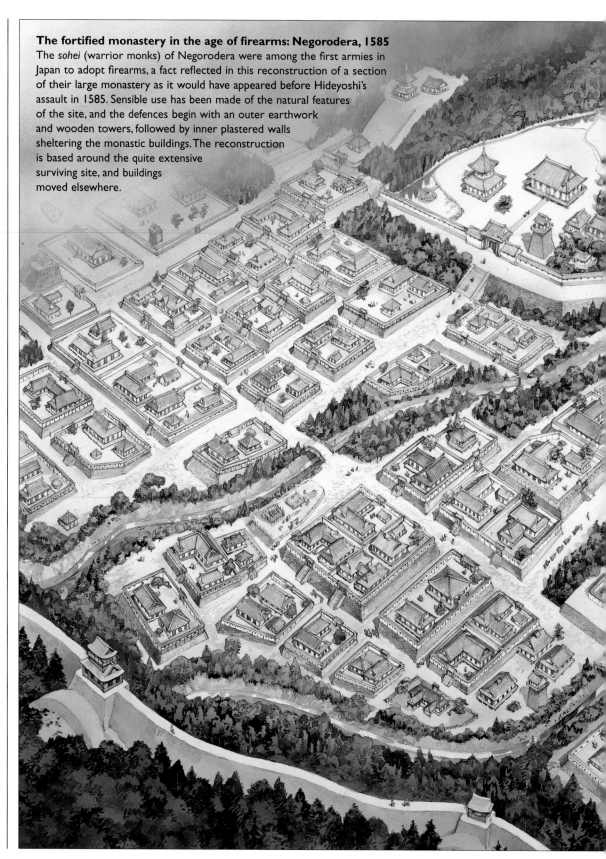

The fortified monastery in the age of firearms: Negorodera, 1585
The *sohei* (warrior monks) of Negorodera were among the first armies in Japan to adopt firearms, a fact reflected in this reconstruction of a section of their large monastery as it would have appeared before Hideyoshi's assault in 1585. Sensible use has been made of the natural features of the site, and the defences begin with an outer earthwork and wooden towers, followed by inner plastered walls sheltering the monastic buildings. The reconstruction is based around the quite extensive surviving site, and buildings moved elsewhere.

The living site

The social structure within a fortified temple

The *sohei* temples were inhabited by warrior monks under the leadership of a *zasu* (chief priest). The 'warrior' element in the expression is fairly self-explanatory, but 'monk' is more difficult to pin down, because although the *sohei* lived in monastic communities, not all of them were monks. Many had indeed taken the vows requisite upon becoming a member of the Buddhist clergy, of which the outward sign was a shaved head, but their armies also included many who had not been ordained. In the words of a recent historian, these included 'minimally educated monks and temple hangers-on, who seem to have been more at home with weapons than with Buddhist scripture'.

The social organization of the inhabitants of a fortified temple of the Ikko-ikki involved a wide range of social classes, resulting from the sect's complex origins in which samurai played an important role. In the early *Sengoku Jidai* there was only a small distinction in practical terms between a low-ranking samurai of modest financial means and a wealthy farmer who might also be a village headman. The latter could not levy taxes, but collected rent from the peasantry and resisted 'real' samurai who attempted to collect taxes from him. The name *jizamurai* is often used for them. To some extent their duties and aspirations were very similar to those of the up-and-coming *daimyo*: they shared a common interest in defending their territory and collecting revenue from it in an efficient manner.

The difference between them occurred in the growth of internal structures. Whereas a *daimyo* aspired towards a vertical vassal structure in a hierarchy of which the *daimyo* was the apex, *jizamurai* had an alternative: the formation of an *ikki*, whereby potential allies joined forces in a mutual protection association. The Ikko-ikki was the largest example in Japanese history of such a creation, but there were many others. For example, in 1485 samurai and 'peasants of all the province of Yamashiro' gathered for a meeting to agree to drive out the troops of the two *shugo* who had been battling over the area. The

The interior of a *sohei* temple is shown in this section of a unique scroll in the possession of Enryakuji. To the right are the chief priest's quarters. Across a corridor lie domestic rooms and a stable. A saddle rests upon a stand in the corridor, while servants bustle about with trays of food. In the stable two horses are firmly tethered.

resulting Yamashiro *ikki* was under the leadership of local samurai, but the organizations of the villages sustained it.

Needless to say, *ikki* formation cut right across the vertical vassal structures that ambitious *daimyo* were trying everywhere to create. In some cases this caused considerable conflicts of interest, because some who were attracted to a *daimyo*'s service might have become accustomed to the horizontal structure of an *ikki* association. Others retained membership of their *ikki* even after they became vassals of a *daimyo*. Weaning them away from such ties was very difficult if the *ikki* involved staunch religious beliefs, such as those that were demanded by Jodo Shinshu. A prime example was the situation that faced the young Tokugawa Ieyasu in the early 1560s. The Ikko-ikki of Mikawa Province were among his greatest rivals, but several of his retainers embraced Jodo Shinshu, so when issues of armed conflict arose such men were placed in a quandary. For example, in the *Mikawa Go Fudoki* account of the battle of Azukizaka in 1564 we read that:

> Tsuchiya Chokichi was of the *monto* faction, but when he saw his lord hard pressed he shouted to his companions, 'Our lord is in a critical position with his small band. I will not lift a spear against him, though I go to the most unpleasant sorts of hells!' and he turned against his own party and fought fiercely until he fell dead.

Through their membership of *ikki*, samurai created alliances beyond their immediate kinship circles under the formal pledge of mutual loyalty. The structure of an *ikki* was therefore broadly democratic, and its rules stated explicitly that any conflict among its members should be resolved at a meeting where the majority decision would apply. Nowhere was this democratic structure more dramatically illustrated than in the ritual that marked the initial formation of an *ikki* or the resolution of a major problem such as a decision to go to war. The visible proof that an agreement had been reached would take the form of a document. Inscribed upon it were a set of written rules to which the members' signatures were added. The signatures were often written in a circle to show the equal status of each member and to avoid quarrels over precedence. Next, a ritual called *ichimi shinsui* (one taste of the gods' water) was celebrated, when the document was ceremoniously burned. Its ashes were mixed with water and the resulting concoction was drunk by the members. The ritual was considered to symbolize the members' like-mindedness that was the outward sign of their solidarity.

Organization and discipline in Jodo Shinshu

Similarly democratic rules applied initially with the Jodo Shinshu's Ikko-ikki, where oaths were signed on a paper that bore an image of Amida Buddha. As it developed, however, the structure of their organization became more hierarchical, with the ruling Honganji on top of the pyramid, intermediate temples in the middle and the local *ko* at the bottom. Contributions, which evolved into annual pledges, came from all levels in the hierarchy. Rennyo also placed his children at major temples and established the *ikkeshu* (family council). It consisted of Rennyo himself, his sons and his grandsons. The *ikkeshu* became the de facto ruling body of Jodo Shinshu following Rennyo's retirement in 1489, and

The gathering of the *monto* to defend Ishiyama Honganji, from *Ehon Shinchokoki*, an illustrated version of the life of Oda Nobunaga. Armour boxes and flags are seen. Note the shaven heads of some of the defenders.

Daily life in the fortified temple: the goeido of Ishiyama Honganji, 1520

The fighting here at Hara has been fierce and two headless female bodies lie against the palisade at the rear. Apart from these poignant details there is considerable information about the defences. The walls, seen here from the outside at the top, are again of solid planking anchored on to the bedrock of the hill, and have the addition of a firing platform in the form of planks laid across strong supports. One defender is kneeling on this rough walkway to loose an arrow over the wall. To his left lies a pile of rocks for dropping through the holes in the walls. A plank laid across a mound of earth gives access to a dropping hole at the left.

continued to serve in that capacity for at least two generations. During the decades following Rennyo's death the *ikkeshu* built up considerable power among the *monto*. To discipline his more unruly followers Rennyo insisted that the *monto* obey the established secular authorities wherever their temples were located. However, the other principle of defence of the faith was also important and, as we have seen, the two often came into conflict. Two formidable sanctions could be applied to miscreants. Excommunication was much feared within a religious-based community, and even execution could be threatened during times of war.

Religious life in the fortified temples

Jodo Shinshu shifted the emphasis of Japanese Buddhism from a monastic-centred organization to the ordinary lives of ordinary people, whose fortified temples housed communities for whom the practice of their religion was a fundamental part of life. The basis of the beliefs of Jodo Shinshu was a purposeful devotion to the worship of Amida, the Supreme Buddha of the Jodo (Pure Land) in the West, who will welcome all his followers into the paradise of the Pure Land on their death. This teaching contrasted sharply with the insistence on attainment of enlightenment through study, work or asceticism stressed by the older sects. To a Tendai monk Jodo Shinshu belief was an illusory short cut to salvation, but Jodo Shinshu welcomed all into its fold and did not insist upon meditation or any intellectual superiority. It also stressed the dire consequences of non-belief as set against the promise of salvation to believers, a dichotomy that led to the Jesuit missionaries dubbing Jodo Shinshu 'the Devil's Christianity'.

Central to the daily life of the temple fortresses was the recital of the *nembutsu*. This brief prayer, *Namu Amida Butsu* (Hail to Amida Buddha), which could be repeated up to 60,000 times a day by devotees, became the motto of the Ikko-ikki armies, who were Japan's 'holy warriors' par excellence. Its *monto* welcomed fighting because their faith promised that paradise was the

Daily life in the fortified temple: the *goeido* of Ishiyama Honganji, 1520

In this plate the inhabitants of Ishiyama Honganji's *jinaimachi* (temple town) are assembling within the *goeido* (founder's hall) that lay at the centre of their fortified community. Buddhist priests of Jodo Shinshu are preparing to begin a service conducted around the *nembutsu* prayer. This cutaway reconstruction is based on a scale model in the Osaka City Museum of History.

immediate reward for death in battle, and nothing daunted them. The devotion associated with the practice only became really apparent when the Ikko-ikki were about to go into battle and the sound of the mass *nembutsu* chilled the blood of their enemies, or when a special service was performed and the *goeido* was packed with worshippers. Lamps twinkled on the pure-gold surfaces of the altar furnishings. The air was heavy with incense and seemed to throb with the responses from hundreds of voices. Just as Shinran intended, to a believer the scene stood as a promise of the western paradise guaranteed by Amida Buddha.

Training for war

Apart from prayer and daily work, preparation for war in the form of military training was the other main activity in the fortified temple, as confirmed by the only description of *sohei* by a western writer. It comes from the European Jesuit missionary Father Caspar Vilela, who has left us a fascinating pen-picture of Negorodera's warrior monk army. Vilela compared the *sohei* to the Knights of Rhodes, but surmised that most of those he saw had taken no monastic vows, because they wore their hair long and were devoted to the practice of arms, their monastic rule placing less emphasis on prayer than on military preparation. Each member was required to make five or seven arrows per day, and to practise competitively with bow and arquebus once a week. Their helmets, armour and spears were of astonishing strength, and, to quote Vilela, 'their sharp swords could slice through a man in armour as easily as a butcher carves a tender steak!' Their practice combat with each other was fierce, and the death of one of their number in training was accepted without emotion. Fearless on the battlefield, they enjoyed life off it with none of the restrictions normally associated with the ascetic life.

Daily life in times of war

When the fortified temple was threatened by an attack the daily life of its community was placed on a war footing. Just as every member of Jodo Shinshu shared fully in its peacetime activities, so did they share in the responsibilities when conflict loomed. Every man, woman and child became involved. All hands were needed, and certainly by the 1580s the experience of a century of war had taught them that if they lost to a samurai army then a massacre of every member of the community would follow.

The first requirement was to concentrate resources on defending that which was most defensible. This meant that outlying farms and fields might have to be abandoned, with the defensive line probably being drawn at the edge of the *jinaimachi*. This was likely to be defended already by some form of perimeter fence or wall, or by natural features such as a river, slope, forest or groves of impenetrable bamboo. There could then be a progressive withdrawal further inside the complex, until a last-ditch stand had to be made within the *hon maru*.

Regardless of the strength of any fortified place in Japan, whether it was a castle or a temple, additions could always be made to its defences when there was an immediate danger of attack. For example, we read in the chronicle *Ou Eikei Gunki* about one castle commander in 1600 who received news of an advance against him and 'immediately replastered the wall and deepened the ditch, piled up palisades, arrows and rice, and waited for the attack'. The archaeological research at Torigoe discussed above found large earthenware storage jars buried in the ground. There was also evidence that when the castle changed hands not only repairs but quite considerable alterations were made to the defences in preparation for a counter-attack. The altered features were no doubt based on the experience of the assault. Those sectors that its captors had found easiest to penetrate now had to be made difficult.

A corner of the defences of Hara. The walls are of solid planking, just like the reconstructed palisade at Torigoe, while outside there appears to be another wall composed of horizontal tree trunks. Inscriptions have been written on the inside of the walls. They are probably prayers to encourage the defenders. Above the planking wall is a wooden framework from which bamboo curtains have been suspended to hide the defenders from outside gaze. The curtains are the worse for wear from the attack, and now hang in tatters. One man is loading his arquebus, while his companion blows on the fuse to get it to glow. In front of them the women and children of the community are preparing a meal for the defenders, with boiled rice being poured into a large wooden tub. Another woman carries a yoke holding two buckets, which may be for water, while a little girl is handing out water in bamboo ladles.

Among the most valuable sources for research into samurai warfare of the Warring States Period are the contemporary painted screens commissioned by participants in various notable battles. Unfortunately, no samurai appears to have regarded the quelling of the Ikko-ikki rabble as being worthy of anyone's brush, so there are no contemporary pictorial records of the Ishiyama War. The scroll in Wakayama depicting Hideyoshi's victory over Negorodera and Ota provides useful information about this war against the last of the *sohei*, but there is no illustration of the activities of the more ordinary members of the two communities. However, only a few decades later the Tokugawa Shogunate was involved in putting down a rebellion that bore remarkable similarities with the activities of the Ikko-ikki. This was the Shimabara Revolt of 1638. The participants on the rebel side were Christian, not Buddhist, but they shared with the Ikko-ikki a similar fanaticism and an almost identical organization under a charismatic religious leader. The Christian rebels – men, women and children, samurai, townsmen and farmers – packed themselves into the dilapidated Hara Castle and held at bay the army of the supposedly all-powerful Tokugawa *shogun*. In the Akizuki Museum there is displayed the contemporary Shimabara Battle Screen, where we see in minute detail a 'citizens' army' defending the castle. Their activities are remarkably similar to those we read about in written accounts of the Ikko-ikki. Certain sections of the screen are reproduced here in the accompanying illustrations with detailed captions.

Operational history

Sohei temples in the Gempei Wars (1180–85)

Sohei were only involved in the first two years of the Gempei Wars. The *Heike Monogatari* gives a brief account of how the *sohei* of Miidera tried to hold off the Taira samurai in 1180:

> At the monastery about a thousand soldier-monks, arming themselves, made a shield barrier, threw up a barricade of felled trees and awaited them. At the Hour of the Hare [6am] they began to draw their bows, and the battle continued the whole day, until when evening came on three hundred of the monks and their men had fallen. Then the fight went on in the darkness and the imperial forces forced their way into the monastery buildings and set them on fire.

This remarkable life-sized diorama in the Heike Monogatari Museum in Takamatsu shows the fallen head of the Great Buddha of Nara after Taira Shigehira's attack on Todaiji in 1181.

The following year the Taira attacked Nara. The monks put up temporary defences and fought so well that Taira Shigehira was forced to risk using the

The fortified temple under attack (I): temporary fortifications outside the Daibutsuden (Great Buddha Hall) of Todaiji, 1181

The attack by Taira Shigehira on the Todaiji of Nara prompted the *sohei* (warrior monks) of Nara to erect temporary defences on the otherwise unprotected site. Here we see the last-ditch stand of the *sohei* outside the hall holding the statue of Buddha that was the wonder of Nara. Wooden shields are their only defence inside the temple compound. This plate is based on written and archaeological evidence of the appearance of the original Daibutsuden, which was much larger that the present-day replacement.

The fortified temple under attack (1): temporary fortifications outside the Daibutsuden (Great Buddha Hall) of Todaiji, 1181

Ganshoji, the rebuilt temple at the heart of the Nagashima complex. A drum tower and a bell tower stand on either side of the gateway through a low but solid wall that make it look well defended. There is a fine *goeido* inside the courtyard, and the whole ensemble is redolent of the idea of a fortified temple.

dangerous weapon of fire. His resulting victory was achieved at the price of the almost total destruction of Kofukuji and Todaiji, including the latter's Great Buddha, so that, in the words of *Heike Monogatari*, 'its full moon features fell to the pavement below, while its body melted into a shapeless mass'.

The siege of Ishiyama Honganji (1570–80)

The events of Nobunaga's longest campaign veered between two extremes: grand strategy designed to isolate the Ishiyama Honganji from any outside help, and a few sporadic but intense periods of bitter hand-to-hand fighting across the fortified temple's walls. The main method of defence for Ishiyama Honganji was the mass use of firearms. In 1570, five years before Oda Nobunaga was to win his famous victory at Nagashino using volleys of arquebus fire, his army, preparing to assault Ishiyama Honganji, were subjected to a surprise night attack involving thousands of gunners. In 1576 Nobunaga led another attack on Ishiyama Honganji that got as far as one of the inner gates. But again mass arquebus fire drove his men back and Nobunaga was himself wounded in the leg. From that time on, strategic considerations dominated Nobunaga's thinking, and over the next four years Ishiyama Honganji was gradually starved of all resources. It surrendered in August 1580.

Nagashima (1571–74)

The position of Nagashima amid sea and swamp determined the ways in which it was defended against Oda Nobunaga's army, and his first attack was a disaster. His mounted samurai began to ford towards the first *waju* (dyked area), only to find that the river bottom was a deep sea of mud. The horses' legs quickly mired, and as the animals struggled many threw off their heavily armoured riders, who were met by a hail of arrows and bullets, causing severe casualties. The shoreline was covered by tall, dense reeds, and as the desperate and demoralized samurai crawled into the reed beds they discovered them to be swarming with more Ikko-ikki arquebusiers and archers. When night fell the defenders realized that the sole survivors of the Oda army were confined within the next *waju*, so the dyke was cut, rapidly flooding the low-lying land and catching the remaining samurai in an inrush of muddy water.

In 1573 Nobunaga, who had benefited from his experience at Ishiyama Honganji in 1570, led an attack on Nagashima spearheaded by thousands of firearms. Unfortunately, a sudden rainstorm rendered most of the weapons inoperable. The Ikko-ikki kept their powder dry, and when they counter-attacked one bullet almost shot Nobunaga off his horse. Nagashima finally fell in 1574 when Nobunaga managed to isolate the sea approaches to it using his fleet. His capture of all the Ikko-ikki outposts on the mainland further cut off Nagashima from help. Waiting until the weather was dry and a suitable wind was blowing, Nobunaga's men simply piled up brushwood against the outer buildings of the Nagashima complex and set fire to the entire place.

One of the storage jars buried in the ground of the *hon maru* of Torigoe, now in the Ikko-ikki Museum in Torigoe.

Torigoe and Futoge (1581–82)

The first attack upon the Ikko-ikki fortified temples of Torigoe and Futoge was made by Shibata Katsuie in the third lunar month of 1581. He captured both and set up a garrison of 300 men, but before the month was out the Kaga Ikko-ikki had recaptured them and slaughtered the unfortunate troops. The attack was part of a general uprising by the *monto* based at these places as well as the fortresses of Matsuyama and Hinoya.

In the 11th month of 1581 Shibata Katsuie and Sakuma Morimasa returned to Kaga and crushed the resistance once again, killing all the *monto* involved. We read that on the 17th day of that month the heads of the ringleaders were sent to Nobunaga's castle of Azuchi and placed on public display. The chronicle names the Ikko-ikki leaders as the father and son Suzuki Dewa no kami and Suzuki Ukyo no shin. Yet in spite of this setback Ikko-ikki resistance continued, and elements of the organization recaptured Torigoe and Futoge once again during the second lunar month of 1582. The defences were rapidly strengthened to face an anticipated third attack by Oda Nobunaga's forces, which materialized on the first day of the third month. The temple castles were taken and destroyed, and this time no chance of resurgence was to be allowed. First, 300 men of the Ikko-ikki were crucified on the river bed, and after this gruesome local display Sakuma Morimasa carried out further suppression with great severity. Over the next three years the inhabitants of the local villages of Yoshinodai and Oso were annihilated.

Negorodera and Ota (1585)

The joint operation against Negorodera and Ota Castle was the last campaign ever conducted against warrior monks. On the tenth day of the third month of 1585, an army of 6,000 men under the command of Toyotomi Hidetsugu, Hideyoshi's nephew, and Hashiba Hidenaga, Hideyoshi's half-brother, entered Kii Province. They crushed four minor outposts, and on the 23rd day of the same month approached Negorodera from two separate directions. At that time the military strength of Negorodera was believed to be between 30,000 and 50,000 men, and their skills with firearms were still considerable, but many had already crossed the river and sought shelter in the more formidable walls of Ota Castle. Hideyoshi's army therefore put into operation the crudest, but often most effective, tactic in samurai warfare for use when the enemy are occupying a large complex of wooden buildings. Beginning with the priests' residences, the investing army systematically set fire to the Negorodera

The armoured monks of Negorodera attempt to salvage some of their treasures as the temple blazes around them during Hideyoshi's attack in 1585. From *Ehon Taikoki*, an illustrated biography of Toyotomi Hideyoshi.

The fortified temple under attack (II): the burning of Nagashima 1574

complex, and cut down the *sohei* as they escaped from the flames. Several acts of single combat occurred between Hideyoshi's samurai and the Negorodera defenders. Some sources tell of Hideyoshi targeting the temple's gunpowder stores with fire arrows so that several explosions helped the process along. Mercifully, the fires were controlled so as to leave part of the temple intact.

Ota Castle was under the command of Ota Munemasa, whose garrison was now considerably increased at the expense of food supplies. In a rerun of his successful campaign against the castle of Takamatsu in 1582, Hideyoshi ordered the building of a dyke to divert the waters of the Kiigawa and flood the castle. A long palisade was begun at a distance of about 300m from the castle walls and packed with earth to make a dam. On the eastern side, which was the Kiigawa, the dyke was left open to allow the waters in. By the tenth day of the fourth lunar month the waters of the Kiigawa were beginning to rise around the castle walls. Heavy rain helped the process along, isolating the garrison more completely from outside help.

Nevertheless, the defenders hung on, encouraged at one point by the partial collapse of a section of Hideyoshi's dyke, which caused the deaths of several besiegers as water poured out. Yet soon hunger began to take its toll, and on the 22nd day of the fourth month the garrison surrendered, although 50 men performed instead a defiant act of *hara-kiri*. The remaining soldiers, peasants, women and children who were found in the castle were disarmed of all swords and guns. Any samurai *monto* were executed out of hand, including 23 of the ringleaders who were decapitated and had their severed heads displayed in Osaka. Their wives were crucified inside the castle grounds. Any farmers were sent back to their masters' fields, thus making the conclusion of the operation a forerunner of Hideyoshi's 'Sword Hunt' of 1588, whereby the non-samurai classes were disarmed and set to work in more fitting occupations.

Although the captions reads 'The Ishiyama War' this woodblock print actually shows the attack on Negorodera in 1585 by Toyotomi Hideyoshi, who appears on the left. In the background is the Ote ike, one of the ponds that provided defence for Negorodera on its western side.

The fortified temple under attack (II): the burning of Nagashima 1574

In this plate we see the culmination of Oda Nobunaga's long campaign against the Ikko-ikki of Nagashima, who have been driven back into the heart of their defences in the river estuary of Ise Bay. Nagashima resembles Torigoe in all but its dramatically different location. Wooden piles have been driven into the muddy shore to build up a firm foundation against floods. But now the main defensive elements of swamps and reed beds have been breached, and flames from piled bundles of wood are starting to lick at the outer walls of Nagashima, which is shown as a predominantly wooden structure of palisades, fences and watchtowers.

Aftermath

To underline his triumph in Kii Province in 1585, Hideyoshi sent the following warning to the Shingon temples on Koyasan that same year:

> Item: The monks, priests in the world and others have not been prudent in their religious studies. The manufacture and retention of senseless weapons, muskets and the like is treacherous and wicked. Item: In as much as you saw with your own eyes that Hieizan and Negorodera were finally destroyed for acting with enmity against the realm, you should be discerning in this matter.

The authorities on Mount Koya were not slow to grasp the point. In 1588, when Toyotomi Hideyoshi enacted his famous 'Sword Hunt' to disarm the peasantry, small landowners or anyone who might possibly oppose him in future, the monks of Koyasan were the first to respond by handing over their cache of arms.

After the destruction of Ishiyama Honganji, Kennyo Kosa sought every opportunity to restore the cathedral of the sect, but only as the religious headquarters of Jodo Shinshu, not as a fortress. Permission was granted after Kennyo sent some of the few remaining Ikko-ikki warriors to harass Shibata Katsuie's rear during the Shizugatake campaign in 1583. In gratitude to the *monto*, Hideyoshi eventually made a parcel of land available in Kyoto in 1589, and the Honganji headquarters were rebuilt there in 1591. This was the same year that Hideyoshi finally achieved the reunification of Japan.

The absence of *sohei* or *monto* from Hideyoshi's last campaigns would seem to indicate that the problem of sectarian violence had been solved forever. But his successor, Tokugawa Ieyasu, who became *shogun* as a result of his victory at Sekigahara in 1600, was not a man to take any chances. Not only did he take steps to emasculate any potential rivals from among the ranks of defeated *daimyo*, he took very seriously any possibility of an Ikko-ikki revival. Ieyasu

The huge *amidado* (Amida Hall, to the left rear) and the *goeido* (Founder's Hall, to the right with two roofs) of Higashi Honganji in Kyoto.

gave high priority to the issue, which he solved in 1602, the year before he was officially proclaimed *shogun*.

The results may be seen by any visitor to Kyoto today. On leaving the station one is struck by the fact that there are two Jodo Shinshu temples, Nishi (Western) Honganji and Higashi (Eastern) Honganji, both of which appear to be the headquarters of the same organization, and which are situated almost next to each other. The explanation is that Tokugawa Ieyasu, who had suffered personally at the hands of the Mikawa *monto*, deliberately weakened Jodo Shinshu by splitting it in two. A dispute between Junnyo, who headed the Honganji and his older brother Gyonyo, provided Ieyasu with the pretext he needed to divide the sect. Ieyasu backed Gyonyo and founded Higashi Honganji to enable him to rival the existing temple, built by Hideyoshi in 1591 and henceforth called Nishi Honganji. This weakened the political power of the sect, leaving it as a strong religious organization, but never again capable of becoming the monk army of the Ikko-ikki.

Jodo Shinshu is today the largest Buddhist organization in Japan, a worthy acknowledgement of the genuine populist roots that Shinran and Rennyo laid down so many centuries ago. However, Toyotomi Hideyoshi had already paid the greatest compliment ever to the Ikko-ikki. He had admired the *monto* for their fine strategic eye, particularly in choosing the sites for their formidable fortified temples. To hold out for ten years against Oda Nobunaga proved that the site of Ishiyama Honganji was a superb strategic and defensive location. Recalling how it had frustrated his master for so long, he chose it as the site for his new headquarters in 1586. Japan's largest castle was established on the site, and in 1615 it required the country's biggest-ever siege using European artillery to crush it. Nowadays it lies at the centre of Japan's second city – the great modern metropolis of Osaka.

The fortified temple sites today

All the fortified temple sites are accessible. They are described as follows, along with other important foundations that shed light on their design and development.

A view from the courtyard of Shorenji in Takayama, showing the *hondo* that dates from 1504.

The drum tower of Shorenji in Takayama. Unlike bell towers, drum towers tend to be enclosed to protect the drum from the effects of the weather.

Nara

Kofukuji, Todaiji and the Kasuga shrine lie next to each other in Nara park. All are very much worth visiting, the Nandaimon of Todaiji and its Daibutsuden (Great Buddha Hall) being the highlights. Beside Kofukuji is the pond of Sarusawa that acted in its defence.

Negorodera

As noted earlier, one has to visit two places to see the surviving buildings of the important Negorodera. The pagoda is still on its original site. The *kondo* is at Daigoji temple to the south-west of Kyoto, easily reachable nowadays since the extension of the underground line out to Daigoji.

Shorenji (Takayama)

One Jodo Shinshu temple contemporary with Ishiyama Honganji, the small Shorenji in Takayama, has survived in its entirety. Located just below the castle hill, the Shorenji was moved to its present position in 1961 to save it from the floodwaters of the Miboro dam. The *hondo* is a very delicate building constructed in 1504. There is also a bell tower, a drum tower and a gate together with a perimeter wall.

Yoshizaki

The site of Yoshizaki Gobo is very well preserved, and is one of the most rewarding places to visit, particularly for anyone

The Rurido (Lapis Lazuli Hall) on Hieizan, the only building to have survived Nobunaga's attack in 1571.

interested in the life of Rennyo. It is difficult to get to by public transport, but easy to access from the motorway. The town also has two museums. The first, the Rennyo Kinenkan, occupies an attractive position on the lakeside and has a garden and tea house. The second is located on the ground floor of Yoshizakiji, a modern temple of quite appalling ugliness. Inside are the originals of some of the most important scroll paintings and documents about Rennyo that exist anywhere in Japan.

The interior of the *goeido* of Koshoji in the *jinaimachi* of Tondabayashi. This is a good example of a small Jodo Shinshu temple hall. The sliding paper doors are attractively decorated with paintings by Kano Hidenobu, a noted painter of the Kano school.

Nagashima

The island of Nagashima lies on the railway line between Nagoya and Ise. One gate of the later Nagashima Castle may be seen, and the rebuilt Ganshoji contains a memorial to the Ikko-ikki. The windswept reed beds that fringe the area are very evocative of the times of the *monto*.

Torigoe

Torigoe is the most interesting place to visit in connection with Ikko-ikki fortified temples. The site is well preserved and restored, and at the foot of the hill is the Ikko-ikki Museum. An Ikko-ikki Festival takes place every August when the villagers dress up in period costume.

Osaka Castle (Ishiyama Honganji)

The site of Osaka Castle contains the site of Ishiyama Honganji. There is a memorial to the Ikko-ikki in the grounds and items relating to Ishiyama Honganji in the museum in the keep. The Osaka Museum of History is situated across the road.

Tondabayashi

Tondabayashi has preserved within its historic centre a glimpse of old Japan. Koshoji has its main gate opening on the east side of the precincts and includes a bell tower and a drum tower on the south and north parts of the precincts respectively. Entering from the main gate, the *hondo* is in front with the reception hall and the priest's living quarters (including a study) on the right-hand side of the main temple. The existing temple was rebuilt in 1638.

Kyoto

The two Jodo Shinshu temples of Higashi Honganji and Nishi Honganji are the nearest one can get nowadays to experiencing what Ishiyama Honganji must have been like. Each has a pair of main halls, but Nishi Honganji's *goeido*, built in 1636, is currently undergoing a ten-year restoration programme due to be completed in 2008. Because Nishi Honganji's *goeido* is temporarily encased within a huge steel hangar, Higashi Honganji is a better bet, even though its buildings only date from 1864. The *goeido*, one of the largest wooden structures in the world, measures 76 by 58m and covers an area of 927 *tatami*.

The temples of Enryakuji and Miidera are easily visited from Kyoto. A cable-car operates from the Kyoto side and a funicular railway from Sakamoto. A visit to Enryakuji involves a lot of walking as the temples are spread out between three main areas. The Konponchudo is the central focus, while the Rurido (Lapis Lazuli Hall) in the Saito area is the only original building to have survived Nobunaga's attack in 1571. The Shakado in Saito was formerly at Miidera.

Glossary

amidado	temple hall dedicated to Amida Buddha
bonji	sanskrit pictographs
goeido	founder's hall in Jodo Shinshu temples
goma	purification and prayer ritual
gomado	temple hall for the performance of *goma*
hara kiri	ritual suicide by cutting the abdomen
hondo	main hall of a temple
hon maru	inner bailey
ikkeshu	ruling family council of the Honganji
ikki	(1) riot; (2) league or organization
jinaimachi	temple town
jizamurai	low-ranking samurai who also farmed
jokamachi	castle town
ko	prayer communities or fraternities
koguchi	barbican
komainu	mythological Chinese dog
kondo	alternative expression for a main hall of a temple
mikkyo	esoteric Buddhist sects
mon	family badge or crest
monto	adherent of Ikko-ikki
nembutsu	literally 'Buddha-calling'; a prayer sequence
ni no maru	second bailey of a castle
Nio	images of guardian gods
raido	public area of a *hondo*
shogun	military dictator of Japan
shoya	village headman
shu	sect of Japanese Buddhism
shugo	*shogun*'s provincial governor
sohei	warrior monk or priest soldier
Sutra	the Buddhist scriptures
tatami	straw mats
waju	dyked community to prevent from flooding
zasu	chief priest

Bibliography and further reading

The following list includes the main works in English to deal with the history and development of the *sohei* and *monto*. Very little is available in English or Japanese on the fortified temples themselves, so much of my research has depended upon fieldwork and site visits, with construction details and layouts being obtained from leaflets and pamphlets available at the sites themselves. For example, the Ikko-ikki Museum next to the site of Torigoe supplies material including the scaled maps that I have used in designing the colour plates.

Adolphson, Mikael 'Enryakuji – An Old Power in a New Era' in Mass, J. P. (ed.) *The Origins of Japan's Medieval World: Courtiers, Clerics, Warriors and Peasants in the Fourteenth Century* (Stanford, 1997) pp. 237–260

Davis, David L. 'Ikki in Late Medieval Japan' in Hall, J. W., and Mass, J. P. (eds.) *Medieval Japan: Studies in Institutional History* (New Haven, 1974)

Fieve, Nicolas, and Waley, Paul *Japanese Capitals in Historical Perspective: Place, Power and Memory in Kyoto, Edo and Tokyo* (London, 2003)

Hayashiya, Tatsusaburo 'Kyoto in the Muromachi Age' in Hall, J. W., and Toyoda, T. *Japan in the Muromachi Age* (Berkeley, 1977) pp. 15–36

Higashi Honganji Temple *Ryodosaikon* (Kyoto, 1997)

Kasahara, Kaguo *Ikko-ikki no kenkyu* (Tokyo, 1982)

Kasahara, Kazuo *Rennyo to Ikko-ikki* (Torigoe, Ishikawa-ken 2002)

Katsuno, Ryushin *Sohei* (Tokyo, 1955)

Kuwata, Tadachika (ed.) *Shinchokoki* (Tokyo, 1974)

McClain, James L. *Kanazawa: A Seventeenth-century Japanese Castle Town* (New Haven, 1982)

McClain, James L., and Wakita Osamu (eds.) *Osaka: The Merchants' Capital of Early Modern Japan* (Cornell, 1999)

Saeki, Tetsuya 'Ikko-ikki saigo no kyoten Torigoe Futoge' in *Maeda Toshiie* (Rekishi Gunzo 'Sengoku Selection' Series) (Gakken, Tokyo 2002)

Solomon, Michael 'The Dilemma of Religious Power: Honganji and Hosokawa Masamoto' *Monumenta Nipponica* 32 pp. 51–65

Solomon, Michael 'Rennyo and the Ikko-ikki' *Transactions of the International Conference of Orientalists in Japan* 21 (1976) pp. 150–155

Sugiyama, Shigeki 'Honganji in the Muromachi-Sengoku Period: Taking up the sword and its consequences' *Pacific World: Journal of the Institute of Buddhist Studies* 10 (1994) pp. 56–74

Tonomura, Hitomi *Community and Commerce in Late Medieval Japan: The Corporate Villages of Tokuchin-ho* (Stanford, 2002)

Turnbull, Stephen *Japanese Warrior Monks AD 949–1603* Osprey Warrior Series 70 (Oxford, 2003)

Weinstein, Stanley 'Rennyo and the Shinshu Revival' in Hall, J. W., and Toyoda, T. *Japan in the Muromachi Age* (Berkeley, 1977) pp. 331–358

Index

Figures in **bold** refer to illustrations

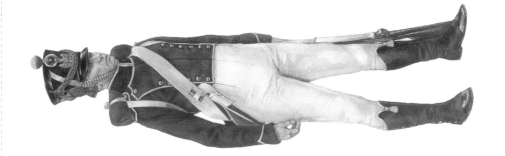

FIND OUT MORE ABOUT OSPREY

❏ Please send me the latest listing of Osprey's publications

❏ I would like to subscribe to Osprey's e-mail newsletter

Title / rank

Name

Address

City / county

Postcode / zip   state / country

e-mail

[FOR]

I am interested in:

❏ Ancient world
❏ Medieval world
❏ 16th century
❏ 17th century
❏ 18th century
❏ Napoleonic
❏ 19th century

❏ American Civil War
❏ World War 1
❏ World War 2
❏ Modern warfare
❏ Military aviation
❏ Naval warfare

Please send to:

North America:
Osprey Direct , 2427 Bond Street, University Park,
IL 60466, USA

UK, Europe and rest of world:
Osprey Direct UK, P.O. Box 140, Wellingborough,
Northants, NN8 2FA, United Kingdom

OSPREY
PUBLISHING

Young Guardsman
Figure taken from *Warrior 22:*
Imperial Guardsman 1799–1815
Published by Osprey
Illustrated by Richard Hook

www.ospreypublishing.com

Knight, c.1190
Figure taken from *Warrior 1: Norman Knight 950 – 1204 AD*
Published by Osprey
Illustrated by Christa Hook

POSTCARD